How
Management
Matters

How Management Matters

Street-Level Bureaucrats and Welfare Reform

Norma M. Riccucci

Georgetown University Press
Washington, D.C.

Georgetown University Press, Washington, D.C.
© 2005 by Georgetown University Press. All rights reserved.
Printed in the United States of America

10 9 8 7 6 5 4 3 2 1   2005

This book is printed on acid-free paper meeting the requirements
of the American National Standard for Permanence in Paper for Printed
Library Materials.

Library of Congress Cataloging-in-Publication Data

Riccucci, Norma.
   How management matters : street-level bureaucrats and welfare reform /
Norma M. Riccucci.
      p. cm. — (Public management and change)
   Includes bibliographical references and index.
   ISBN 1-58901-041-8 (pbk. : alk. paper)
   1. Public welfare—United States. 2. Public welfare administration—
United States. 3. Bureaucracy—United States. 4. Welfare recipients—
Employment—United States. I. Title. II Series.
   HV95.R515 2005
   361.973'068—dc22

                                                           2004023154

Ai miei cari cugini, con molto affetto

Olinto and Popa Riccucci

Pasquale and Gina Riccucci

Franco and Maria Manciati

Contents

Tables and Figures

Figures

Acknowledgments

I gratefully acknowledge the U.S. Department of Health and Human Services for its generous funding for the larger research project from which this book emanates. I also wish to thank the other senior researchers of the project, Marcia Meyers, University of Washington, and Irene Lurie, University at Albany. Certainly, some of the ideas expressed here came about as a result of that collaboration. Some of the earlier co-authored work is also cited.

I also wish to express my deep gratitude to the Rockefeller Institute of Government in Albany, New York, for its generous support. In particular, the Rockefeller Institute's director, Richard P. Nathan, and the director of the Federalism Research Group, Thomas L. Gais, provided invaluable input, feedback, and research assistance on the larger project. They are gratefully acknowledged.

A number of colleagues provided very helpful feedback on drafts of this manuscript. They include first and foremost the series editor at Georgetown University Press, Beryl A. Radin; Steven Maynard-Moody; David H. Rosenbloom; Frank J. Thompson; Marc Holzer; and Jun Seop Han. In addition, several support staff are thanked for all their hard work: Miriam Trementozzi, Maria Augostini, Rebecca Corso, Melissa Rivera, Madelene Perez, and, from the Center for Legislative Development in Albany, New York, Nan Carroll, Clare Yates, and Dawn Guinan.

Finally, I wish to extend thanks to all those who participated in the study, from the students who conducted most of the field work to all of the commendable public servants—administrators, managers, and front-line workers—who gave willingly and freely of their time for interviews and observation.

Preface

Scholars of public administration and public policy have devoted an enormous amount of attention to the importance of public management in the operation of public bureaucracies. An extensive body of research has demonstrated and established that management has a direct impact on the efficacy of organizations. However, by comparison, there has been very little research focusing on the effects of public management on street-level bureaucratic behavior. This is an important issue because street-level bureaucrats possess an extraordinary amount of power in influencing how public policies are implemented. Some studies show that bureaucrats or workers at the street level tend to be guided by pervading work norms, customs, and shared experiences. But what exactly has the role of public management been on the work behavior of street-level bureaucrats? This important question represents a critical gap in the literatures of public management, public policy and street-level bureaucrats.

This book examines how and where public management in government organizations matters. The context for examining this question is the 1996 welfare reform law, officially called the Personal Responsibility and Work Opportunity Reconciliation Act (PRWORA), which sought to change the behavior of welfare staff as well as of their clients. In particular, the law sought to change the work functions and behaviors of street-level welfare workers from one of eligibility determination to one of employment coach or counselor with the ultimate aim of moving welfare clients off assistance and into jobs. Thus, welfare reform provides an auspicious environment for examining where and how public management matters.

Specifically, this book looks at the welfare reform law of 1996 to investigate the effects of management on street-level bureaucratic behavior in welfare offices. It also examines the significant role that street-level bureaucrats play in the implementation of welfare reform. The book further addresses the role of public management in changing the system of welfare under the reform law as well as management's impact not on policy outcomes, but on organizational outputs in welfare offices, defined here as ensuring the delivery of welfare benefits and services to eligible clients. This is not to say, of course, that public management has no effect on policy outcomes. Rather, the data available for the research presented in this book are not sufficient to answer that question.

CHAPTER ONE

How Can Management Not Matter?

A question that has been a perennial source of debate in the public administration, public management, and public policy literatures is whether management makes a difference in the operation and performance of government organizations. The intuitive response to this is, "Of course it does." Indeed, there is an immense body of literature addressing the importance and significance of public management and leadership[1] for public sector organizations.[2] This body of research, addressed later in this chapter, demonstrates the positive impact that public managers and leaders have on the quality and productivity of their organizations and on the delivery of public services.

Although there is abundant evidence that management makes a difference in the operations and productivity of public and private sector bureaucracies, there is another body of literature purporting that management *does not* matter. This research paints a very pessimistic picture of the ability of administrators and managers to redirect the juggernaut of modern society—large, entrenched bureaucracies. Some scholars argue that bureaucratic systems make it extraordinarily difficult for management to change the direction, nature, or culture of their organizations.[3] Some argue that this is particularly the case at the front lines of service delivery, where workers possess a good deal of discretionary power, thus making them more difficult to manage or supervise.[4] There may be one level of bureaucratic activity, then, where management has less of an impact: street-level bureaucrats.

In addition to whether or not public management matters, the question is often asked: "What exactly does public management have an impact *on*?" This question has significance for both the public administration and public policy communities, but each tends to view the issue from a different perspective. The public policy community generally looks more closely at policy implementation from the standpoint of policy outcomes—a speeding ticket, food stamps, drug rehabilitation programs—and the process or factors leading to such outcomes. The public administration community may also be interested in management's impact on policy outcomes, but it is also concerned about the effect of management on organizational outputs—ensuring that the actual work of the organization gets done, such as making sure that services and benefits are delivered.[5] Public administrative scholars also tend to be more interested in questions of accountability, constitutionality, and democracy with respect to service delivery.[6] Recognizing the constraints that management faces in the public sector (e.g., lack of resources), managerial efforts may sometimes be more directly connected to organizational outputs, which depend heavily on the ability of managers to make decisions, allocate resources and priorities, set up and maintain reporting systems, and so forth.[7]

How Can Public Management Make a Difference?

The purpose of this book is to examine not only whether public management matters, but how it matters and the *level* at which it matters. The context of bureaucracy plays an important role here: management may matter in terms of leadership, broad management reforms, and policymaking, and even in terms of "setting the stage" for office politics and practices.[8] However, at the front lines of service delivery, where workers may be guided by pervading work norms and customs as well as by shared experiences and knowledge, street-level bureaucrats often perform their job duties and functions while relying very little on management directives. This is not to suggest that street-level workers are explicitly engaging in subversive behaviors or are cavalierly flouting the rules and regulations that permeate their work.[9] Rather, workers at the front lines often pursue goals that are consistent with their work norms, familiar routines, professional standards, and socialization experiences.

The research presented in this book seeks to bridge or reconcile the conflicting bodies of literature on whether management matters. It illustrates that management in terms of managerial reforms and administrative practices may have a greater impact at the broader levels of organization—the more "macro," structural, and behavioral levels of the organization or bureaucracy itself. Management may also have a greater effect on organization outputs as compared with policy outcomes. But at the "micro," front-line levels of bureaucracy, work customs, professional norms, and socialization often define work behaviors, making it more difficult for managers to affect the actual work of their staff.[10] The research will further explore, however, whether and in what ways front-line workers are at least open to management guidance and directives. In this sense, the research can foster our understanding of the behaviors of street-level bureaucrats with the ultimate aim of developing management strategies for directing their behaviors toward achieving desired organizational outcomes.

Conceptual Framework

Because this book seeks to bridge different streams of literature or research on public management and policy, it is guided by several different theoretical frameworks: (1) the functions of public management, (2) the role of street-level bureaucrats in the public policy process, and (3) the significance of work norms and culture in employee behavior. Discussed briefly below, each will be addressed more fully in its respective, relevant chapter.

Critical Functions of Public Management

There is an immense body of research demonstrating the important impact that public management has had on the delivery of public policies, programs, and services.[11] But management means different things to different researchers. For example, some studies point to the positive effects of public management from the standpoint of administra-

tive or managerial capacity or arrangements, such as networking capabilities, program structuring, or interorganizational coordination.[12]
Such research might examine the degree to which broad managerial
and policy reforms can change the structural and institutional arrangements of public policy delivery systems.

Another body of research focuses on public management from a behavioral perspective, examining how attributes, behaviors, and practices
of managers and leaders (e.g., open, participatory styles of leadership)
can affect public policies.[13] Thus, management can assume a host of
distinctive meanings. For the purposes of this study, management is
conceptualized in terms of both administrative capacity and managerial practices and behaviors.

As noted earlier, it is also important to ask on what exactly public
management has an impact. Some studies examine management's impact on policy priorities, organizational environments, or policy outcomes. Other studies focus more on organization outputs. This study
examines the impact of public management not on policy outcomes,
but on organizational outputs, defined here as management efforts to
ensure that the multiple and conflicting goals of the organization are
met and, ultimately, that benefits and services are delivered to the
agency's clients.

Street-Level Bureaucrats

The classical model of the public policy implementation process suggests a top-down, hierarchical approach. The process, as many have suggested,[14] has been depicted roughly as it appears in figure 1.1. This
somewhat static view of the policy implementation process may illustrate the broad elements of the process, but it does not account for the
important role that public management plays in the process, nor for the
role of street-level bureaucrats.[15] It also fails to account for the importance of organizational outputs.

Elmore refers to policy implementation at the street levels of bureaucracy as "backward mapping;" it is a bottom-up as opposed to a
top-down approach.[16] In fact, street-level bureaucrats play an essential

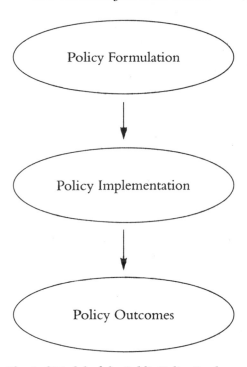

Figure 1.1. The Classical Model of the Public Policy Implementation Process.

and somewhat paradoxical role in the implementation process. It is at the street level where policy delivery may be most critical for social programs, because the actions of front-line workers have substantial and sometimes unexpected consequences for the *actual* direction and outcome of benefit programs.[17] A more dynamic depiction of the policy implementation process that interfaces the concerns of both public administration and public policy would look something like that which is presented in figure 1.2.

Work Norms and Culture

A third stream of research also informs the current study: the effects of work norms, customs, and the culture of the profession or the job itself on the behavior of street-level workers.[18] Front-line workers develop a set of shared, unwritten rules that consciously and often unconsciously drive their work behaviors. Thus, even if workers lack

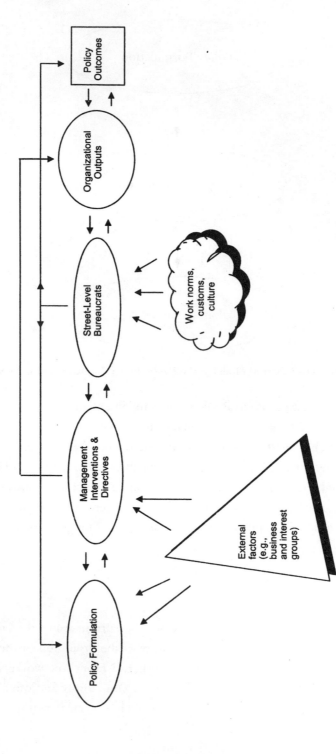

Figure 1.2. Management, Street-Level Bureaucrats, and the Policy Implementation Process.

formal professional training in a specific policy area such as social work, the socialization process and the dictate of "informal organization" guide street-level bureaucrats in their delivery of welfare services, or more broadly, in their "profession." As Sandfort points out:

> Through daily experiences, staff generate collective schema that help them to understand their work and efficiently utilize organizational resources. In the implementation of social policy, these factors create parameters that staff use to interpret future events and justify their actions.[19]

The Context

The context for examining the question of whether and how public management matters is the 1996 welfare reform law, the Personal Responsibility and Work Opportunity Reconciliation Act (PRWORA), which sought to change the behavior of welfare staff and their clients.[20] One of the most compelling social policy questions of the last several decades has been, "How can the welfare system in this nation be reformed?" The 1996 law represents the most sweeping legislation to welfare since the federal entitlement program Aid to Dependent Children (later renamed Aid to Families with Dependent Children, or AFDC) was created in 1935. In particular, PRWORA eliminated federal entitlements for cash assistance (AFDC), replacing it with Temporary Assistance for Needy Families (TANF), which allows state officials to design and deliver their own programs and services for cash aid, child care, and employment.

Through a variety of management and policy reforms, the law sought to move welfare clients off welfare and into jobs. Inherent in the legislation and the ensuing policy was an effort to change the work functions and duties of welfare workers from one of eligibility determination to one where front-line staff would coach and counsel welfare clients to find jobs. For these reasons, welfare reform is a natural experiment in the question, "Can management reforms change the manner in which front-line workers implement public policy?"

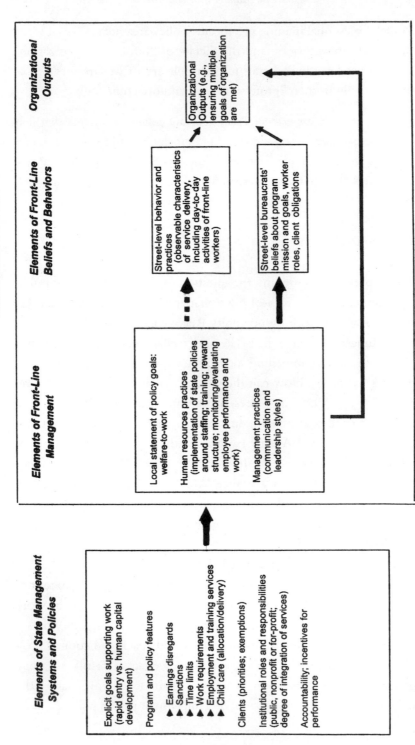

Local Welfare Office

Elements of State Management Systems and Policies

Explicit goals supporting work (rapid entry vs. human capital development)

Program and policy features
▲ Earnings disregards
▲ Sanctions
▲ Time limits
▲ Work requirements
▲ Employment and training services
▲ Child care (allocation/delivery)

Clients (priorities; exemptions)

Institutional roles and responsibilities (public, nonprofit or for-profit; degree of integration of services)

Accountability; incentives for performance

Elements of Front-Line Management

Local statement of policy goals: welfare-to-work

Human resources practices (implementation of state policies around staffing; training; reward structure; monitoring/evaluating employee performance and work)

Management practices (communication and leadership styles)

Elements of Front-Line Beliefs and Behaviors

Street-level behavior and practices (observable characteristics of service delivery, including day-to-day activities of front-line workers)

Street-level bureaucrats' beliefs about program mission and goals, worker roles, client obligations

Organizational Outputs

Organizational Outputs (e.g., ensuring multiple goals of organization are met)

Figure 1.3. Conceptual Model for Impact of Public Management on Street-Level Bureaucrats and Organizational Outputs.

The role of management in street-level bureaucrats' implementation of welfare reform goals is the setting of this study and a focal point of this book. Street-level bureaucrats or front-line workers are defined as those workers in welfare offices who have direct, face-to-face contact with TANF applicants or clients. Both qualitative and quantitative data are used to offer rich evidence and insights into the effects of management in terms of capacity and practices on the delivery of welfare policy and services.

The Model

Figure 1.3 provides a conceptual framework for examining the potential impact of public management on the operation of welfare at the local level of government and on the performance of street-level bureaucrats.[21] In terms of how and in what context management matters, figure 1.3 can best be viewed in its various components or segments. For example, "elements of state management systems and policies" represents administrative capacity or, more specifically, the broad managerial and policy reforms at the state level for implementing welfare reform. This book begins, in chapter 2, by first examining the broad federal reforms to welfare and then looks at exactly how states have changed their welfare systems in response to the federally mandated goals.

As the model further illustrates, these broad, state-level reforms could potentially affect the "elements of front-line management" in local welfare offices. This is addressed in chapter 3. Based on these broad, macro-level reforms at the state level, it is expected that local welfare offices will make certain administrative and managerial adjustments, including adopting "welfare-to-work" goals.

A closer look at management capacity, practices, and behaviors in local welfare offices (i.e., the "elements of front-line management") will also indicate whether and how managers have prepared their offices for the new goals of welfare reform. For example, it is expected that local managers will convey the welfare-to-work priority to front-line or street-level workers in their agencies but, at the same time, also

ensure that client processing remains a key job function of the workers. In this sense, management capacity and behavior are linked to organizational outputs, or ensuring that the multiple goals of the organization are met. These issues are also addressed in chapter 3.

As seen in figure 1.3, the study also asks whether management in
terms of administrative capacity and behaviors in local welfare offices
affects either the actual behaviors or beliefs of front-line workers in
terms of service delivery. These issues are addressed in chapters 4 and 5.
It is expected that management factors such as managerial and leadership styles, organization structure, and human resources practices will
influence at least front-line workers' *beliefs* about the mission of their
welfare agencies. However, as indicated by the dashed line in figure 1.3,
the impact of the "elements of front-line management" on the actual
behaviors of street-level bureaucrats is expected to be more tenuous
where factors such as work norms and customs may be more consequential. Also examined are the effects of management and street-level
workers on organization outputs.

As noted earlier, the primary focus of this book is on how management affects organization outputs and the behaviors and beliefs of
street-level bureaucrats in their delivery of welfare benefits and services, the issues labelled in figure 1.3 as "local welfare office." Thus, it
focuses on organizational outputs, not policy outcomes. That is to say
it does not address the causal effects of either management or street-
level workers on actual policy outcomes. Certainly, inferences can be
drawn here, but outcome data (e.g., Do TANF clients get jobs? What
is the rate of TANF approvals or denials?) were not made available for
this research, thus precluding an examination of how street-level workers or management influence policy outcomes.

Research Approach and Methods

Data for the research were collected in 1998 and 1999 in four states:
Georgia, Michigan, New York, and Texas. The four states were pur-
posely selected to maximize variation in policy, administrative struc-

Table 1.1. Welfare Office Sites, by Urbanicity.

Site Type	Georgia	Michigan	New York	Texas
Urban	Atlanta: Fulton County (Northwest, Southwest)	Detroit: Wayne County (Glendale/ Trumbull)	Albany County	Dallas: Grand Prairie, Masters
Rural	Bibb County (Macon)	Hillsdale County		Denton County
Suburban		Macomb County (Sterling Heights)	Suffolk County, Long Island (Smithtown Center)	

Source: Rockefeller Institute of Government, Albany, New York, Front-Line Management Study.

tures, and political culture.[22] And although the four states may not be entirely representative of the country as a whole, those selected were seen as innovators in welfare reform. In addition, the states selected had adopted explicit policies to promote employment and, at the same time, reduce welfare reliance.

In terms of administrative and staffing structure, Michigan and Texas illustrate centralized or state administered welfare systems, New York administers welfare services and programs predominantly at the county level, and Georgia has a mix of state and county administered welfare services.

Within each of the states, data were collected from two to three local or county sites in order to provide variation in community context (e.g., urban, rural, or suburban), management practices, and client characteristics (see table 1.1). A site is defined as the local public welfare agency. Ability to gain access to the local welfare offices was also a criterion for state and local site selection.

Data were collected from four primary sources: (1) content review of agency documents and forms; (2) face-to-face semi-structured interviews with agency administrators, managers, supervisors, and a sample of front-line workers; (3) on-site paper-and-pencil surveys of front-line staff (see appendix A for copy of survey); and (4) direct observations of the "encounters" between front-line staff and TANF applicants or clients.[23] Excerpts from the transcripts are woven into the various chapters to provide examples of what actually takes place in worker–client meetings, as well as to illustrate the potential impact of management (e.g., in the in-take process or application for assistance, as seen in chapter 3). Appendix B provides more comprehensive information on the data, the data collection process, and the sample for this study.

The 1996 welfare reform act resulted in a good deal of research on the implementation of welfare reform policy in this nation. However, few of these studies have taken up the questions of how management and policy reforms have influenced practices at the front lines of service delivery, and how public managers may have contributed to these practices and to the delivery of new welfare reforms. These issues are addressed in this book.

CHAPTER TWO

Ending Welfare as We Knew It

*"If you like laws and sausages, you
should never watch either one being made."*
— Otto von Bismarck

During his 1992 presidential campaign, Bill Clinton popularized the notion of "end[ing] welfare as we know it." It was a vague yet prophetic concept, one that would, in fact, materialize, thoroughly changing the face of welfare in this nation. Just six months into his administration, President Clinton set the wheels into motion: he named a twenty-seven-member task force to develop a welfare reform plan. Bruce Reed, deputy assistant to the president for domestic policy, was named to lead the effort along with the team of David T. Ellwood, assistant secretary for planning and evaluation, U.S. Department of Health and Human Services (HHS), and Mary Jo Bane, HHS assistant secretary, Administration for Children and Families.[1] Over the next few years, Democrats and Republicans alike, in both the the Senate and the House of Representatives, introduced a panoply of welfare reform bills (see appendix C).

This chapter begins by examining the broad effort at the federal level to reform welfare, culminating in the Personal Responsibility and Work Opportunity Reconciliation Act (PRWORA). It then looks at exactly how states have changed their welfare systems in response to the federally mandated goals.

The Beginning of the End to Welfare

In June of 1994, President Clinton unveiled his plan for welfare reform: the Work and Responsibility Act. The proposal called for $9.3 billion in additional federal funding over five years and sought to impose a mandatory work requirement on Aid to Families with Dependent Children (AFDC) recipients born after 1971 after two years of seeking work. The proposal would expand the JOBS Program—passed in 1988 to help AFDC recipients avoid long-term welfare dependency by providing education and training—and strengthen regulations regarding paternity establishment and child support.[2] The bill would require minors to live at home as a condition of receiving aid. All but $2.1 billion of the new funding would be offset through reductions in entitlements, such as Supplemental Security Income (SSI). Two weeks later, the Clinton welfare bill was officially introduced in both the Senate and the House.[3]

After two years of congressional wrangling—and the inclusion of a provision that would end the entitlement status for cash assistance—on August 22, 1996, President Clinton signed the federal Personal Responsibility and Work Opportunity Reconciliation Act into law. Following decades of frustrated attempts to "reform" and redirect the welfare system, the law for the first time changed the organizing principles and goals of the welfare system, from the provision of cash assistance to the promotion of employment and the reduction of welfare reliance (see appendix D).[4] The most dramatic change was the elimination of federal entitlements for cash assistance (AFDC) and the imposition of a time limit on assistance. Under Temporary Assistance for Needy Families (TANF), which replaced AFDC, states are no longer required to provide assistance as an entitlement or to adhere to the numerous federal eligibility rules created under AFDC. This gives state officials substantial new authority to design and deliver their own cash aid, child care, and employment services.

Along with this authority, Congress gave states very specific new performance requirements. States were directed to impose more stringent work requirements on aid recipients and, at the same time, restrict TANF-funded assistance to a lifetime maximum of sixty months for

Table 2.1. Change in TANF Caseloads in the United States, 1993–2000 (in thousands).

Caseload Type	1993	1994	1995	1996	1997	1998	1999	2000	Sept. 2002	Change 1993–2002 No.	Percent
Families	4,963	5,053	4,963	4,628	4,114	3,305	2,734	2,208	2,024	2,939	−59
Recipients	14,115	14,276	13,931	12,877	11,423	9,132	7,455	5,781	4,995	9,120	−65

Source: U.S. Department of Health and Services, The Administration for Children and Families, www.acf.dhhs.gov/news/stats/newstat2.shtml. Date accessed: June 8, 2003.

any one individual. By the year 2002, states were required to have half of all TANF recipients placed in work or community services activities. Although this goal was not fully realized, caseloads dropped nationwide by almost 60 percent between 1993 and 2002 (see table 2.1). This was an important goal of welfare reform. The actual reasons for the drop in caseloads fall beyond the scope of this book, but certainly the drops are in part attributable to PRWORA. Not to be overlooked is the robust economy of the late 1990s, which would explain much of the increase in employment.

In addition, under welfare reform, states are also no longer required to provide access to education, training, job placement assistance, work programs, or child daycare assistance. In short, the reforms to the welfare system did indeed change welfare as we knew it.[5]

The Key Provisions of PRWORA

There were four key provisions of the federal welfare law:

- **Block grants.** The federal government provides each state an annual block grant, fixed for a period of six years, which is based on the state's previous AFDC spending level. For the fiscal year 1997, federal TANF funds ranged from $21.8 million in Wyoming to over $3.7 billion in California.[6]

- **Welfare-to-work.** The states must require able-bodied recipients to participate in work or work-related activities (e.g., job search). States must require adults in families receiving TANF to participate in work or work-related activities after receiving assistance for twenty-four months, or sooner as defined by state law. New applicants to TANF are generally required to attend an orientation on work requirements and responsibilities under TANF. Clients are required to sign the Personal Responsibility Agreement (PRA), which states that the client agrees that TANF is temporary, that TANF is a work program, and that it is the client's responsibility to get and keep work. To avoid penalties, states must meet minimum participation rates. As of 2002, the minimum participation rate for one-parent families was 50 percent. Those exempt from the work requirements generally include disabled recipients or caregivers and "payees" (e.g., grandparents who receive financial assistance on behalf of the dependent grandchild).

- **Time limits.** States must impose a cumulative five-year time limit on TANF-funded cash assistance for families with adults. Up to 20 percent of a state's caseload may be exempt for reasons of hardship. Families with no adult receiving assistance (known as "child-only" cases) are not subject to this limit. States may choose to continue providing cash assistance using state funds.

- **Reducing out-of-wedlock pregnancies.** The federal law requires the U.S. Department of Health and Human Services (HHS) and the states to establish goals and take action to reduce the incidence of out-of-wedlock pregnancies.

Within these broad parameters, as well as guidelines issued by HHS, states were provided with a good deal of flexibility and discretion in developing their welfare laws. For example, states could set forth their own criteria regarding who is eligible for assistance and at what levels. States now had the ability to deny assistance altogether to noncitizens, minor teen parents, drug felons, or those deemed able to work, and they can now also impose time limits lower than five years.[7] Earnings disregards, which allow a certain amount of income from employment to be disregarded in terms of benefit calculation, are also within the purview of the states. States were also now able to set guidelines covering participation in work activities, the range of acceptable work activities, qualifications for good cause exemptions from work, and the termination of cash grants for noncompliance with state program requirements. The provisions of the new child care block grant are similarly broad. In 1996, Congress also consolidated a number of categorical child care entitlements that had been linked to AFDC into a single measure called the Child Care and Development Block Grant (CCDBG). Like welfare, child care is no longer an entitlement for poor families but rather a discretionary service that is funded jointly by the federal and state government but managed by the states.

Basically, states receive a block grant that they can draw on, and they are free to set policies on such important aspects as eligibility, the duration of benefits, the type of providers who will be reimbursed, the level of reimbursement, and the level of parental co-payments. States may also transfer large amounts of money from the TANF block grant to child care. While devolving authority for the management of child care subsidy programs to the states, the federal child care law continued the existing structure of public child care provision, in which most public funds are distributed as vouchers to be used by parents to purchase private services. Outside of support for infrastructure investments as a part of quality improvement initiatives, the federal block grant provides few resources or incentives for state government to intervene in the overwhelmingly private, market-driven mechanisms through which child care services are actually provided.

The reauthorization of TANF was to occur by September 31, 2002, the date that PRWORA officially expired. However, Congress failed to reach an agreement on a five-year reauthorization bill or even a scaled-down three-year extension proposed by a group of state-level officials. Instead, Congress approved in November of 2002 a short-term extension which allowed states to receive their quarterly TANF block grants in January of 2003. This temporary extension ran through March 31, 2003, the point at which Congress was charged with passing a full-fledged reauthorization bill for PRWORA. As of this writing (October 2004), PRWORA has yet to be reauthorized, and TANF continues to operate on short-term extensions.

Welfare Reform in the States

In conformity with the federal TANF law, states developed welfare reforms with a strong emphasis on employment and independence. Governors and state legislators sent strong signals that a work-based system would be a central goal for their state (see, for example, Nathan and Gais 1999). To encourage and support work, states strengthened the linkage between welfare and work agencies and devoted more funds to child care and transportation. A brief summary of the unique provisions of the reforms adopted by each state included in this study follows.

Texas

When George W. Bush became governor of Texas in 1994, one of his priorities was to reform the state's welfare program. In fact, overhauling welfare was one of the main planks of his first campaign for governor. Within his first year as governor, Bush was successful in getting a bill through the Texas legislature that dramatically changed the welfare system in Texas by making work an immediate priority for low-income families receiving AFDC. By 1995, Texas received federal authority to implement Achieving Change for Texans (ACT), its waiver-based welfare reform initiative; implementation of the new law began in May of 1996.[8]

By 1997, after the passage of PRWORA, the Texas Department of Human Services (DHS) launched its welfare-to-work program, "Texas Works." The vision statement for Texas Works was "your independence is our success," and front-line staff were expected to help TANF clients identify barriers to employment and find resources that would help them achieve economic self-sufficiency. The state agency responsible for delivering employment services to TANF clients is the Texas Workforce Commission (TWC), created in 1995 to oversee and provide workforce development services to job seekers and employers in Texas. Consolidating twenty-eight workforce training programs, the TWC contracts with nonprofit workforce development boards across the state, which, in turn, contract with other agencies, private or nonprofit, to deliver employment services to TANF clients. For example, in one of the sites included in this study—Denton—the TANF work program is run by the North Texas Human Resource Group, a nonprofit organization that is a contractor of the North Central Texas Workforce Development Board. In the other two sites included in the study—Masters and Grand Prairie—a private, for-profit agency, Lockheed Martin, contracts with the Dallas County Workforce Development Board to provide employment services for TANF clients. Interestingly, however, the workers for Lockheed Martin are former workers of the state's Department of Human Services (DHS), the agency responsible for the delivery of TANF and related benefits and services.[9] As a condition of winning the contract, Lockheed Martin was required to hire those workers who would have otherwise been laid off from the DHS.

As governor of Texas, Bush wanted to turn over most of his state's welfare services to private firms. Everything from cash assistance to food stamps and Medicaid would have been run by profit-making businesses. Companies that had bid to run welfare services included Lockheed Martin, IBM, Electronic Data Systems, and a subsidiary of Arthur Andersen. The Clinton administration rejected the plan, arguing that needy families should not have to rely on profit-seeking companies for decisions affecting cash, food stamps, and Medicaid eligibility and benefits.

Governor Bush also supported "faith-based" welfare initiatives, where agencies would contract with religious organizations to provide welfare-to-work and other related support services. In fact, he issued an executive order encouraging state agencies to use the federal welfare reform law's "charitable choice" option to contract with religious organizations. As president, George W. Bush has continued to support linkage with faith-based organizations for the delivery of support services under welfare.

The "work first" initiative in Texas was implemented with the intention of diverting families at the outset from going on welfare. It is promoted in part as a "moral" response to prepare the needy for independence; it reinforces "personal responsibility" and emphasizes the message that looking for work must precede the application for cash benefits.[10]

Specifically, the new in-take process at Texas's DHS starts by diverting families that apply for public assistance to a resource room to look for a job before their applications are accepted. If they are unsuccessful in their efforts to find a job, they can then apply for aid. Then, once their application is thoroughly reviewed and accepted by a DHS Texas Works Advisor (TWA), it is "pended" until the TANF applicant attends a workforce orientation run by the relevant work or employment agency (e.g., Lockheed Martin). Once the individual can show evidence of a bona fide effort to find work, his or her application for aid is finally processed. This diversion process can take several weeks. While it is happening, the potential welfare applicant is both diverted from public aid and sent for more intensive workforce development services.

Under Governor Bush, Texas substantially altered its welfare and workforce systems from the state-level down to the local service providers starting in 1995, well before any of the federal reforms were fully conceived. In fact, the attention given to welfare policy by Bush and his lieutenant governor, Robert D. Bullock, represented a precedent in Texas law and for policymakers in general.[11] As he campaigned for the presidency in 2000, Governor Bush characterized himself as a "compassionate conservative," a description meant to evoke a kinder version of Republican without committing him to any specific action. On welfare, for example, Bush said, "It is conservative to reform welfare by insisting on work. It is compassionate to take the side of charities and churches that confront the suffering which remains."[12]

Georgia

In 1986, Georgia launched its Positive Employment and Community Help (PEACH) program. The precursor to TANF in Georgia, PEACH was a comprehensive employment and training program with various support services for AFDC clients. It was administered by Georgia's Division of Family and Children Services (DFCS)[13] along with the state's departments of labor and technical and adult education and its Job Training Partnership Act. Through contractual arrangements,

PEACH provided education, training, child care, and transportation for welfare recipients, with the goal of moving them into jobs.[14]

Almost ten years later, in 1995, DFCS, under the leadership of Michael Thurmond, changed the focus of welfare from income maintenance (i.e., cash benefits and services) to employment in a program known as "Work First." Immediate job placement of welfare recipients became the primary goal of DFCS, thereby diminishing PEACH's focus on long-term training and education. Seventy-three counties in Georgia were named Work First sites in July 1995 and given greater freedom to develop plans for moving toward an employment-oriented service style.

Legislation submitted by Governor Zell Miller and passed by the General Assembly established a family cap in which a parent who had received benefits for twenty-four months would receive no additional benefits for another child. An employment requirement was instituted that sanctioned able-bodied recipients with no children under 4 who quit or refused to take a full-time job. Teen mothers were to live with a parent or guardian, and children were required to be up-to-date on immunizations. Child support enforcement measures were strengthened to make it easier to establish paternity and collect payments.

In January of 1996, Work First was implemented statewide. It shifted the emphasis of DFCS from approving cases and distributing welfare checks to putting AFDC recipients to work. Finding a job became the primary objective of each welfare applicant, and as a result almost 12,000 applicants were diverted from the welfare rolls by finding a job while their paperwork was being processed.[15]

With passage of PRWORA, Georgia continued its welfare policies with the goal of "workfirst." Other major provisions of Georgia's law included time limits and a family cap whereby TANF recipients who have another child after ten months on assistance will not receive an increase in cash assistance due to the birth of an additional child. In addition, Georgia's TANF program has a "two strikes and you're out" rule. A first sanction may be imposed for violation of a work requirement or the client's failure to fulfill the conditions of the personal work and responsibility agreement. This first sanction carries a 25 percent reduction in the recipient's TANF grant. The recipient has 90 days to clear the first sanction. If the recipient fails to do so, a second sanction is imposed, which results in termination of assistance.[16]

The agency charged with administering TANF, as with AFDC, is DFCS. In 1997, Georgia's Department of Labor was contracted to provide employment services, namely, job skill assessment and job placement, both of which were formerly provided by DFCS.

Although policymaking around welfare remains largely in the province of state officials, in reality county agencies are far more involved in that they have wide latitude in defining and implementing their programs. Moreover, county DFCS operations are allowed to co-venture with local governments in programming and service delivery. For example, Fulton County DFCS, which services Atlanta, works with the Fulton County government to deliver benefits from the county government's General Assistance program. And Bibb County DFCS, which services Macon, works with county government, local schools, and area nonprofits to provide a child-care center. In this sense, Georgia represents a "mixed model" of welfare service delivery, with both state and county involvement in defining the contours of welfare reform.

A critical problem that has been identified in Georgia around the implementation of welfare reform is that counties have reported low basic skills as a significant barrier to employment, ranging from 25 percent of the case load in Rockdale County to 40 percent in DeKalb County and 80 percent in Fulton County. Limited English-language proficiency was also a problem in some counties, ranging from 35 percent in Fulton County to 40 percent in DeKalb County. Substance abuse was also identified as a problem in Georgia counties. On average, counties estimated that 20 percent of their caseload has a substance abuse problem.[17]

Michigan

Welfare reform began in Michigan when Governor Engler's plan "To Strengthen Michigan Families" was implemented in 1992. The plan, authorized by thirteen different federal waivers outlining twenty-one "policy innovations," emphasized strengthening family functioning and "increasing productive output."[18] As the economy in Michigan improved, however, and more jobs became available, the emphasis shifted to "Work First . . . and Foremost." The plan was expanded in 1994 with twenty-seven new initiatives and more waivers, and clients were required to participate in Work First! initiatives to receive benefits. The 1992–1994 reforms have been described as being entirely executive branch–dominated, and, according to one observer, the legislative branch was generally not consulted about the federal waivers.

In keeping with its aggressive approach to reform, the state of Michigan enacted two welfare reform bills in March of 1996 in anticipation of the federal TANF block grant program. The two bills, in effect, have become the state's TANF reform measure. Its overarching goal is summed up by how welfare reform is commonly referred to in Michigan: "Work First!" Immediate job placement is emphasized over human capital investment with the ultimate goal, in the words of Governor John Engler, of encouraging "independence and self-reliance, while building self-esteem."[19] The formal welfare program in Michigan is known as the "Family Independence Program."

The politics surrounding the enactment of a welfare reform act in Michigan deserve brief attention. For example, when the welfare reform bills were being developed, outside groups were not consulted or convened to deliberate or to mobilize support for changes to Michigan's welfare law. Although external advisory groups were established to address four key areas—cash assistance, childcare, child protection, and Medicaid—the 1995 welfare reform package was ultimately drafted by a small task force consisting of four Republican legislators and the director of the Department of Social Services (DSS), Gerald Miller. The bill was based almost entirely on rules that had been drafted and implemented by the governor and the DSS between 1992 and 1995. Moreover, the bill created a large measure of discretion for the DSS, the agency charged with overseeing welfare programs in Michigan at the time by allowing it to issue rules and policies that would ultimately embody welfare reform. Members of the legislature who opposed the bill, mainly Democrats, did not want an executive-level agency to wield this degree of power over welfare policy.[20]

When the welfare bills were enacted, both chambers of the Michigan legislature were controlled by Republicans. And Governor Engler, also a Republican, had pushed for welfare reform that emphasized work since his election in 1990. Democrats complained about the lack of public input, asking why a Senate subcommittee on yard waste held hearings across the state, while changes to the state's welfare system merited no hearings whatsoever.[21]

The Democrats in the legislature were also dismayed by an item in the bill that called for an eighteen-month exemption from Michigan's Administrative Procedure Act.[22] This unprecedented exemption would not only allow the DSS to develop and implement new administrative rules for welfare quickly without adhering to the act, it would also avert or circumvent lawsuits from being filed by advocacy groups challenging the administrative rules.

Democrats further complained about the "railroading" of welfare reform by Republicans, who were motivated to move quickly in order to have the first welfare reform bill in the country. This, according to the House speaker, would "keep Michigan as a leader in welfare reform."[23]

The bill passed in record time: less than a month, whereupon it was signed into law by Governor Engler. One advisory group member had this to say about the overall process: "The governor's office already knew what they wanted and pretty much stuck with their plan regardless of what the [advisory] groups had to say. . . . The groups were more of a cover than having real input in policy."[24]

The goals of the state's reform bill, Public Act 223 of 1995, included "Efficient, fair, cost-effective administration of the family independence program" and "provision of family independence assistance to families willing to work toward eventual self-sufficiency." Although not expressly stated as a "goal," the act also declared that the "new" welfare in Michigan was expected to "achieve more efficient and effective use of funds for public assistance . . . reduce dependency . . . or . . . improve the living conditions and increase the incomes of individuals receiving public assistance."

The Michigan law also divided oversight of welfare reform between two administrative agencies: the Family Independence Agency (FIA), which replaced the Department of Social Services, and the cabinet-level agency Michigan Jobs Commission (MJC).[25] The FIA was granted a great deal of latitude to "perform the duties imposed in" the act. The act explicitly granted the FIA the authority to "develop policies to establish income and asset limits, types of income and assets to be considered for eligibility, and payment standards for assistance programs administered under" the act.

On the employment side, the MJC was given responsibility and resources to deliver all employment services for TANF clients, from employment assessment to job placement. The MJC is largely free of the detailed procedural oversight to which the FIA is subject. The MJC was given responsibility for the Work First! initiative in 1994, and for the JOBS program (formerly run by the DSS) and the EDGE program (formerly run by the Department of Education) in the fiscal year 1994–95.

New York

Beginning in 1995, welfare policy in New York State underwent a series of major shifts. With an emphasis on work and personal responsibility, the state instituted a host of administrative changes that would have a profound effect on the delivery of social services. A year later, with the passage of PRWORA, New York was provided with the additional flexibility needed to pursue a welfare reform program that would move welfare clients from welfare to work and self-sufficiency. The welfare system evolved from one of income maintenance to one focused on nonpublic assistance income support such as employment and child support.

In August of 1997, Governor George Pataki signed into law the New York State Reform Act. Its main goal was to help welfare clients to reduce their dependency on public assistance by helping them find jobs. The 1997 Welfare Reform Act authorized a major restructuring of the administration of welfare at the state level. Prior to the act, the

DDS was responsible for the administration of public assistance, social services, Medicaid, child support, and welfare-to-work programs. The act eliminated the DSS and replaced it with two new offices—the Office of Temporary and Disability Assistance (OTDA) and the Office of Children and Family Services. It also shifted Medicaid to the Department of Health, welfare employment programs to the Department of Labor, and child support enforcement to the Department of Taxation and Finance.

Under the Act, the "Home Relief" category of public assistance, guaranteed to those qualifying for aid under the New York state constitution, was also replaced by the Safety Net program. Adopted in 1938, article XVII, section 1 of the state constitution mandates state/local general assistance to "aid, care, and support the needy" and for "the protection and promotion of the health of the inhabitants of the state." Thus, those families exhausting their five years of TANF would be guaranteed assistance in accordance with the state constitution. Safety Net assistance is a mix of cash and noncash benefits. Also, single adults and childless couples can qualify for Safety Net assistance.

In New York, welfare is state-directed but locally administered. The financing is intergovernmental; counties and New York City assume 25 percent of cash benefits provided to TANF clients, and 50 percent of those for the Home Relief/Safety Net recipients. In addition, New York's 57 counties and New York City are required to share the non-federal costs of Medicaid.[26]

At the county level, where much of the welfare policy is actually implemented and delivered in the form of services, there is much less fragmentation. For example, in both Suffolk and Albany counties, sites included in this study, it is the Department of Social Services that is responsible for all income maintenance functions. In Suffolk County, the county Department of Labor provides the work-related activities required of TANF clients. In Albany County, the work function is theoretically integrated into the county DSS. However, there is a separate cadre of workers that provides only the employment services; the income maintenance services are provided by other workers not involved in the delivery of work-related services.

In sum, state officials moved quickly to reform their welfare systems in response to the federally mandated goals of PRWORA. These state-level policy and managerial reforms, as will be seen in later chapters, have been critical to the implementation of welfare reform. But despite the new goal of supporting work or "welfare to work," the former purposes of the welfare system also remain. As in AFDC law, TANF's purpose is to provide assistance to needy families so that children can remain with their parents or relatives. And when government distributes money, the demand for accountability leads it to focus on accuracy and scrutinizing client's income and needs. In these ways, the law maintains the old tension between the goal of assisting parents so they can care for their children and the goal of discouraging welfare receipt through pressure to work and a concern for accuracy. As Hasenfeld has argued, the welfare reform law has created a

> vast incompatibility between administering welfare—determining income eligibility, setting a grant amount and monitoring for cheating—and providing employment and social services—identifying client needs, locating appropriate services, and helping clients change their behavior.[27]

Because PRWORA seeks to embrace these dual and conflicting goals, it may have resulted in ambiguities and complexities over performance standards for agencies and the front-line workers.

CHAPTER THREE

The Important Role of Public Management in Welfare Reform

A good deal of research has demonstrated the importance of public management in the delivery of public policies, programs, and services.[1] The preponderance of this scholarship relies on a qualitative or case study approach and represents critical empirical work on the impact of effective management on government performance.

This chapter begins by reviewing this body of literature on public management and the positive effects it has on the delivery of public services. It then points more specifically to the important role management plays in the delivery of welfare services under PRWORA. Referring to the model in chapter 1, it illustrates how management in terms of administrative capacity (e.g., program structure, broad-based managerial reforms) at the state level could affect "elements of front-line management" in local welfare offices. It then looks more closely at management practices, behaviors, and capacity in local welfare offices to ascertain whether and how managers have prepared their offices for the new goals of welfare reform. For example, have local managers conveyed the welfare-to-work priority to front-line or street-level workers in their agencies? Are managers at the same time ensuring that client processing remains a key job function of the workers? In this sense, are management capacity and behavior linked to organizational outputs or to ensuring that the multiple goals of the organization are met? These issues are addressed in this chapter.

How Does Management Matter?

As the literature illustrates, public management has been conceptualized in different ways. For example, some of the research points to the effects of public management from the standpoint of administrative or managerial capacity or arrangements, such as interorganizational coordination, program structuring, networking capabilities, and physical capital.[2] Ingraham and Donahue define management capacity as "government's intrinsic ability to marshal, develop, direct and control its human, physical, and information capital to support the discharge of its policy directions."[3] They go on to say that "governments with more management capacity have the ability to perform better than governments with less management capacity, all else being equal."[4]

Relying on Ingraham and Donahue's research, Coggburn and Schneider examine the effects of management capacity on public policy priorities.[5] They specifically find that those states with greater management capacity in terms of physical, human, and information capital promote policies that tend to benefit the public at large (e.g., police protection) as opposed to more particularized groups (e.g., reflected in such programs as employment security).

Another body of research defines public management from a behavioral perspective, examining how the attributes, behaviors, and practices of managers and leaders can impact public policies.[6] Denhardt, for example, in examining characteristics of successful managerial performance, illustrates the critical role that public leaders and managers play in improving the quality and productivity of their organizations.[7] Meier and O'Toole illustrate that managerial quality, as measured by, for example, merit pay awarded to school superintendents in 1000 Texas school districts, is positively correlated with enhanced government performance, as measured by such indicators as improved standardized test scores and an increase in school attendance.[8]

Related literature in the behavioral sciences also examines the effects of management and supervision specifically on work behaviors and attitudes.[9] These studies also show that particular styles of management and leadership (e.g., open, participatory styles) lead to more

positive work behaviors and attitudes.[10] Hutchison, Valentino, and
Kirkner, for example, report that managers with a higher interpersonal
and participatory orientation had a positive effect on worker commitment toward organizational goals.[11]

Research on the New Public Management, with its focus on "reinventing government," suggests that adopting businesslike management
practices will enhance government performance and will also help
change the culture of bureaucracy.[12] Importantly, however, this body of
research is not supported by empirical evidence. Moreover, critics of the
New Public Management provide compelling reasons why this approach
to managerial reform is likely to *impede* the ability of a democratic form
of government to deliver services to the American public effectively.[13]

The body of research specifically examining the impact of public
management on welfare and child care systems also indicates that effective public management can improve the delivery of welfare services.[14] For example, Behn's important study of the efforts of the Massachusetts welfare bureaucracy to shift the focus of local welfare offices
toward supporting and promoting employment among welfare recipients tells us that "leadership counts." He states: "To achieve public purposes, leadership counts. . . . What affects the performance of a welfare,
training, and employment program? Leadership by the department's
top managers."[15]

Likewise, Mead points to the role of management and leadership
as well as organizational reform in bringing about change in Wisconsin's welfare bureaucracy. As he points out, effectiveness (e.g., improved
enforcement of child support) "does not just happen. It takes high levels of administrative quality and resources."[16] Programs that are better
managed and led proved to be more successful.

In sum, there is a host of literature demonstrating that public management, defined in a variety of ways, positively affects the delivery of
government services. The following sections point to the important
role managerial efforts have had in the delivery of welfare services
under PRWORA. As noted, for the purposes of this study, management is defined in terms of both administrative capacity (e.g., program

structure, broad-based reforms, human resources practices) and managerial behavior (e.g., management styles).

Public Management and Welfare Reform

As described in chapter 2, several broad-based policy and management changes were instituted by state-level officials and administrators in response to PRWORA. These broad-level managerial and policy restructurings did, in fact, change the face of welfare across the nation. Whether the changes are viewed positively or negatively depends on how one interprets the goals of welfare reform: delivering cash assistance, diversion from cash assistance, or promoting employment.

Broad Managerial and Political Reforms

Perhaps the major reform feature that has influenced the delivery of welfare services has been a macro-level change in the organizational structure of state welfare bureaucracies. With the exception of Albany County, every state included in this study placed the employment or work function (i.e., helping clients find jobs) into an existing labor department or, as in Michigan and Texas, newly created labor or work agencies. Thus, the oversight of welfare reform has been divided between two administrative agencies: one for income maintenance service delivery and a completely separate department or agency specifically required to deliver all employment services—from employee assessment through job placement.[17]

Even in Albany County, where the work function is theoretically integrated into the county DSS, employment services for TANF clients are performed as a separate operation from the income maintenance function. An entirely separate cadre of workers provide *only* the employment services; the income maintenance services are provided by other workers not involved in the delivery of work-related services.

The policy decision to place the responsibility for the delivery of employment services in an organizational unit separate from the income maintenance delivery unit may be one of the most critical moves affecting the welfare bureaucracy. At the outset, it places the task of helping TANF clients find jobs *not* with front-line TANF or welfare workers, who historically performed eligibility determination tasks or functions, but rather with specialized workers in a separate employment agency, whose job is and has always been to help a particular class of clients (e.g., the unemployed or former prison inmates) find jobs. Thus, the welfare *system* was set up so that workers in specialized agencies traditionally focusing on employment would be responsible for helping clients find jobs. This certainly sent a signal to street-level workers in the welfare offices that helping clients find jobs is neither within their purview nor expected of them.

In addition, the abolishment of entitlement to aid, along with the imposition of time limits and the mandatory work participation requirement, serve to deter welfare applicants or clients, particularly in the early stages of the application or recertification process. As noted in chapter 2, PRWORA eliminated federal entitlements for cash assistance and also gave states broad authority to develop their own systems for delivering cash as well as other benefits. States are no longer required to adhere to the vast federal eligibility requirement rules created by AFDC. Time limits also deter welfare applicants and, to a certain extent, bind the hands of welfare workers.

The work-first or mandatory work requirement also serves as a deterrent. The added step of having to go to a separate office—which is not always in close physical proximity to the welfare office—to participate in work or work-related activities (e.g., job search) for a prescribed, set number of hours per week (e.g., 20 to 30) may cause clients to give up their quest for aid, dropping out of the system altogether.[18] The signal of work first is, in effect, being sent by organizational cues or "processes" and not by the welfare workers. In short, these broad-based policy and management reforms have changed the nature of welfare and also place certain constraints on the behaviors of front-line workers.

The In-Take Process

Another very critical impact of policy and management reforms can be seen in the in-take process, or the actual application form itself, which is a tangible expression of the will of management. The in-take process also serves as a deterrent to welfare. Managers at the state level designed these forms and the forms impose certain requirements on the worker, which in part drive the worker-client interaction or encounter and also place some, albeit minor, constraints on worker discretion.[19] The front-line worker has an obligation to record client responses on the in-take form and ensure that the welfare applicants or clients provide certain information, present various forms of verification (e.g., electric bills, rent receipts), as well as sign the Personal Responsibility Agreement (PRA), which states that the client agrees that TANF is temporary, that TANF is a mandatory work program, and that it is the client's responsibility to get and keep work.

The in-take process and the application form vary across states, but the one common feature to all sites is that it is cumbersome and time-consuming. Moreover, workers' efforts to ensure that certain requirements are met (e.g., the signing of the PRA) can detract from the client's needs being addressed or even heard.[20] That is to say, workers sometimes become so preoccupied with filling out the forms that they may not hear, and thus not respond to, the needs of the applicant or client. Wallace Sayre called this the "triumph of techniques over purpose."[21]

The following transcript from an encounter at the Division of Family and Children Services (DFCS) at the Southwest Fulton Office in Atlanta, Georgia, illustrates how the applicant's needs get lost in the worker's obligatory processing of the in-take form. The TANF applicant is in her late twenties or early thirties, has two children, and suffers from the disability of schizophrenia. She has just moved to Atlanta from Connecticut. In all likelihood, she will need some level of assistance for life, but the worker proceeds to have her sign the PRA and grants her a *one-time* waiver from the work requirement.

WORKER: Tell me why you came to Atlanta.

APPLICANT: Mental illness that caused me to come home and be around family members. [*hands over a letter from her physician in Connecticut.*]

WORKER: Have you applied for social security disability?

APPLICANT: I don't know where to go.

WORKER: The social security office. You live over on Campbellton Road?

APPLICANT: Yes.

WORKER: Since you're in here today, I think the closest place is MLK. You can go there and apply for social security disability.

APPLICANT: I thought it was in here, too.

WORKER: Is this your home?

APPLICANT: Yeah. Do you know how much that is—social security?

WORKER: If it's just plain old social security, it's $520 a month, plus you get Medicaid.

APPLICANT: Will that drop it out of here?

WORKER: No, you'd still get TANF for your children, we'd just drop you off the case. You'd get $235 for them, which would help with income, until you're mentally able to go back to work. Since right now you're not mentally able to go to work, there's a one-time exemption available. I'm going to go ahead and use that until you get a doctor's statement that you can go to work.

[*Later*]

APPLICANT: How soon could I get [Medicaid], because Tiffany's tooth is loose.

WORKER: OK. We'll see. This form states you're not a victim of domestic violence. This is your one-time exemption saying you won't have to work until you learn about disability from social security. This is the family cap rule. I'm going to explain it to you, but I want you to read it before signing. It says if you receive TANF for 24 straight months and then have another baby it won't be added to your TANF. You can have as many babies as you'd like, but the government won't pay for it. This is the child support form—it releases information to child support enforcement. This is the interview form we finally got printed. It's everything I asked you. I need you to sign and date for me. This is your Personal Responsibility—it has those things I told you about going to PTA. It requires you to sign and date. [*signs and dates*] You have Medicaid this month?

APPLICANT: No.

WORKER: In Connecticut?

APPLICANT: They stopped that, too.

WORKER: It won't stop until April 30th. So, technically, you're not eligible in Georgia until May 1st. But if it were me and my child needed attention, I'd take her to the doctor and try. They may not take a Medicaid card from Connecticut, but they might.

In another case, the applicant clearly needs food on an emergency basis and continually brings the interview back to this issue, but the worker spends more time counseling the applicant on family planning. The applicant is 18 years old, has two children, and is pregnant. She is applying for TANF, Medicaid, and food stamps at the DFCS, Northwest Fulton Office in Atlanta, Georgia. Because the applicant is under 22 and living at home, she is not eligible or cannot qualify for food stamps on her own.

WORKER: Who do you live with?

APPLICANT: My mother.

WORKER: What I can do is, because you're 18, I can't let you apply for food stamps, your mother'd have to apply. But I can apply you for TANF and Medicaid.

APPLICANT: OK.

WORKER: Now, did you finish high school?

APPLICANT: No.

WORKER: Are you working on your GED?

APPLICANT: No. I want to, but I can't because of child care.

WORKER: Well, you'll have to, because it's mandatory if you're applying for TANF.

APPLICANT: I don't have money.

WORKER: We'll supply you with support services, including child care.

APPLICANT: OK.

WORKER: You have some ID on you?

APPLICANT: Yes.

WORKER: I'll need a picture ID, social security card. Now usually—do you know about our TANF program? Usually the young ladies and young men who come in to apply here, usually first we put them into job search. But because you're under 21, you're mandatory to do education, and get your GED. And then after that, you'd do job search.

APPLICANT: OK. Do you have a food program?

WORKER: Only thing I could do is give you a referral for food. What you need to do is call that number.

APPLICANT: OK.

[*Later*]

WORKER: You pregnant?

APPLICANT: Yeah.

WORKER: Girl, were you on some kind of birth control?

APPLICANT: [*shakes head*] I shoulda been.

WORKER: You right, you should've been. You already got two children. And you haven't finished high school. How pregnant are you?

APPLICANT: One month and two days.

WORKER: You gonna be using birth control after that?

APPLICANT: Yeah. I wanna get my tubes tied.

WORKER: It's your choice. You live with your mother. She have any other children living there?

APPLICANT: Yeah, there's three of us.

WORKER: Three total?

APPLICANT: Four total. I didn't know that—I didn't know you had to be that age to apply for food stamps.

WORKER: Yes, unless you live alone. Your mom receive any assistance?

APPLICANT: She works.

WORKER: That's probably why she can take care of her children. Like you need to.

APPLICANT: I was working, when my sister was here, she'd watch them. Then she left and I had to stop working.

WORKER: Well that's gonna be a problem—child care. You didn't think about that.

APPLICANT: I do now.

WORKER: You will have to deal with it. Stop having babies.

APPLICANT: Most definitely.

[*Later*]

WORKER: Why'd you get fired [from your last job]?

APPLICANT: Drugs.

WORKER: What kind of drugs?

APPLICANT: Marijuana.

WORKER: You were smoking marijuana?

APPLICANT: Yes, ma'am.

WORKER: You still smoking?

APPLICANT: Yes, ma'am.

WORKER: What I got to do, put you in a program?

APPLICANT: No.

WORKER: What are you gonna do?

APPLICANT: I'm trying to straighten.

WORKER: OK, you need to go to the life skills class.

APPLICANT: Is this [food bank] close by?

WORKER: What you need to do is call the number and they'll give you referrals of where you need to go. I'm going to talk with one of the employment services workers, I'll be right back. . . . OK, we got all kinds of stuff to do for you. What's gonna happen is I'm gonna have to make a referral to CPS [Child Protective Services]. And they're gonna help you get yourself together. About the skills of life. Also, I'm gonna give your name to our substance abuse folks. But remember, to get TANF, you're gonna have to do school. All these things you're gonna have to do to get your life together.

APPLICANT: Y'all give emergency food stamps?

WORKER: No emergency food stamps.

APPLICANT: How long it gonna take [to get food stamps]—five days?

WORKER: Yeah. Now it's gonna include her wages, her income. That's it. Now somebody will contact you about classes and the drug program and you need to get in school.

In one encounter, in the DFCS office at Bibb County, Georgia, the worker insisted on explaining the rules around the family cap at length, even though the applicant had had her tubes tied:

WORKER: . . . in regards to family planning and birth control.

APPLICANT: I got my tubes tied.

WORKER: Well, we still have to tell you about it. When TANF came into place they put something called family cap into place.

The worker proceeded to provide a lengthy explanation of the family cap, which places financial penalties on TANF clients for having additional children, and then asked the applicant if she needed a referral to the health clinic.

In one last example from a Dallas, Texas, Office of the Department of Human Services, a client clearly shows her frustration with having to follow the rules-driven in-take procedure, especially since her previous application for aid, and the accompanying verification forms, cannot be found.

WORKER: How have you been supporting yourself?

APPLICANT: Oh I used to clean, just temporarily I would clean different people's houses and do odd little jobs for them.

WORKER: OK, we're gonna have to verify everything, but I'll make a list of everything I'm gonna need from you. So basically your sister is providing for you, pampers and everything?

APPLICANT: No. She is not.

WORKER: Who is doing that?

APPLICANT: No one right now. That's why I am here asking for help.

WORKER: OK.

APPLICANT: No one is doing it right now. I was in Mahare, Texas, and my sister had a brain tumor. I get so tired of telling the same story. I mean you have all that right there in that file.

WORKER: No, ma'am, I don't. This is what's in your file.

APPLICANT: But what happened to it?

WORKER: I guess you were in Mahare, Texas?

APPLICANT: No, I already filed, I did one here. All the same information. I'm tired of going over and over and over it. Kayja!! [*calls child*] And me having to sit and wait forever. That's ridiculous. They put me through the same thing over and over and over. But anyway, my sister had a brain tumor. She is unemployed at this time.

WORKER: OK.

APPLICANT: She was, she worked up until November 3rd. OK. They removed a brain tumor. I came here to stay with her.

WORKER: OK.

APPLICANT: OK. She live alone. Her and her two kids. We're struggling. That's why I am here asking for help.

WORKER: OK. So. . . .

[*Later*]

WORKER: And what happened?

APPLICANT: That's where a lot of information is started.

WORKER: And you provided it?

APPLICANT: Yes, we did. We brought it up here. I got a call into Austin right now. As we speak. I've called and I talked to, I don't know, I guess that's your district office, and they're gonna be getting back to me because we brought all that information up here. Last time we spoke with a Kathy somebody.

WORKER: OK. So if you didn't provide the information.

APPLICANT: We did.

WORKER: You still have to provide it. Do you have a receipt?

APPLICANT: A receipt for what? What information are you asking for?

WORKER: For the same information they asked you for when you came in. . . . All I see it's gonna do is for us to do policy and if I have to ask you for forms you still have to provide them.

APPLICANT: Have I refused to do that?

WORKER: Uh uh.

APPLICANT: Have I refused to do that?

WORKER: Not with me you haven't.

APPLICANT: OK, I mean it was the way you said it, like I. . . .

WORKER: I mean I'm gonna go back and look in her case to see what else she needed.

APPLICANT: I don't mind supplying you with whatever you ask me for.

WORKER: OK, great.

APPLICANT: But the way you just said it's like, I'm not giving you what you need. We gave everything they've asked for and nobody has gotten back with us.

WORKER: OK.

APPLICANT: But then we didn't put it in Kathy's hand either, we left it at the front desk, so there's no telling.

WORKER: Did you get a receipt for it?

APPLICANT: Uh, no. No, we just made copies of it.

WORKER: OK. I'll ask Kathy, you know, if she has the information. So I'll have to ask if she sent it down to us to see what's going on. That's all. They don't. You know we have to go [through] policy and all that.

APPLICANT: I understand that.

WORKER: So the fact that you called Austin doesn't mean that, you know, we have to jump.

APPLICANT: No, I'm not asking nobody to jump. I just want Austin to know that there's a lot of people in this office that's not doing what they're paid to do. So I wanted to make that clear, because obviously they don't know it.

WORKER: OK.

APPLICANT: Come on, Kayja.

WORKER: Right now are you applying for their household?

APPLICANT: No, just me.

WORKER: And your baby?

APPLICANT: Right.

WORKER: OK, I need her birth, her social security card.

APPLICANT: Oh, I don't have it.

The encounter lasted for an hour and twenty minutes with a decision of "pending" for TANF, Medicaid, and food stamps until the client provided additional information and documentation to the caseworker.

These encounters represent just a few examples of how the management-driven application and in-take process have affected worker-client interactions as well as potential outcomes. Under welfare reform, new rules were created, which resulted in an enormous amount of new paperwork. Workers are required to get the applicants to sign various forms and enter into various agreements (e.g., the PRA), which often obscure and eclipse the substantive concerns of the clients (i.e., finding or receiving some form of assistance, including emergency food supplies). The process itself has become exceedingly laborious and convoluted. If the goal of welfare reform is to get people off assistance, then the in-take process itself is certainly helping to fulfill that goal.

In sum, management in terms of capacity has led to fundamental changes in the welfare system. This is seen in the broad-based policy and management reforms as well as the in-take process itself. And front-line workers, their discretionary powers notwithstanding, can do little to alter the implementation or outcomes of these actions, decisions, and reforms.

Management and Organizational Outputs at the Local Level

Management capacity and accompanying policy actions within the local welfare offices are also critical to organization outputs, or ensuring that the multiple goals of the organization are met and that, ultimately, services and benefits are being delivered at the front lines of welfare bureaucracies. The priorities managers set for their offices, goal communication, human resources practices, and management styles or behaviors can all potentially influence the delivery of welfare services.

Importantly, administrators, managers, and supervisors of local welfare offices operate within certain bureaucratic constraints that can affect their ability to influence program or policy implementation. For example, state civil service rules preclude them from reclassifying jobs or from developing reward and disciplinary systems to motivate or punish their employees. In addition, training programs for local welfare workers are often developed and administered by the parent state agency to ensure uniformity and reliability in the content and delivery of the training.

Nonetheless, county welfare managers and administrators do enjoy a degree of latitude in terms of organizational outputs, especially in those states that call for county-administered welfare programs. Local management is responsible for ensuring that the work of the agency gets done—it must set the tone and stage for the delivery of services by clearly establishing and articulating the goals of their offices, ensuring that the functions of their offices are performed effectively, and developing management and leadership styles that will foster the ability of the front-line workers to achieve the specified goals.

Local Statement of Policy Goals

As illustrated in table 3.1, local administrators and managers indicate that the priorities of their welfare offices reflect the goal of putting welfare clients to work. In virtually every site included in this study, local managers and administrators indicated in face-to-face interviews that "work first" was the priority for their agencies. Only in one site, Suffolk County, New York, did local administrators explicitly indicate that deterrence or stopping people from coming on welfare was their goal under welfare reform.[22] As one official from Suffolk County explained: "There is some sense that when the worker explains all the referrals, they discourage applicants,"—that is, from coming on TANF.

One county manager in Wayne County, Michigan, stated that "the goal is to get as many people as possible employed. Our goal is for all

Table 3.1. Statement of Formal Goals of Welfare Reform, by Officials from Sample States or Counties.

Goal Level	Georgia	Michigan	New York	Texas
State		Strengthen Michigan families; Work First; self-sufficiency, financial independence, and mutual responsibility		Work First; diversion
County	Bibb: Work First and preventing TANF applicants from "crossing the line" to receive welfare		Suffolk: Front-end deterrence; fraud reduction	
	Fulton: Work First		Albany: Work First; front-end deterrence	

offices to have 100% employment, so the federal participation rate . . . doesn't mean as much to us." Similarly, in Macomb County, one manager said, "The message we are trying to get out is that, from the day you apply, we are mutually trying to make you independent. What is it we have to do to get you there—day care, transportation, removing barriers. It's a little bit of stick and some carrot."

In Bibb County, Georgia, one administrator commented that "we divert close to 70 percent of the people from even going on welfare. . . . [We try] to keep them from crossing the line [into TANF]." In Fulton County, a similar goal is espoused: "It's about working with people. Getting their incomes up. Moving them to work."

In the three welfare sites in Texas, managers and supervisors consistently stated that "the policy from Austin has been work first; go to work and get a job." One admitted that "our goal has been to help clients find jobs before their time limits are up. . . . But the jobs don't always pay enough to help a family get by."

One front-line supervisor in a Texas welfare office, however, pulled no punches:

Texas didn't want anyone on welfare. So they have made it as hard as possible to get it. . . . [It's] about getting people off welfare. It's no secret, it's in the papers. But that is politically incorrect, so they say it is about getting people jobs. Welfare reform just wants to get clients off the rolls. It doesn't really help them.

Interestingly, the signals actually *received* by front-line staff about the goals of their offices are somewhat dissonant. In the face-to-face interviews with front-line workers, some stated that the message they hear from managers and supervisors is that the priority for their offices is welfare-to-work. One front-line worker in Hillsdale, Michigan, for example, stated that "getting people to work" was the goal. Another stated that "I try to motivate them to go to work. Maybe that's why my interviews are longer. I try to plant seeds. I try to plant ideas."

A street-level worker from another Michigan welfare office said that "the focus now is to help them get off welfare and get jobs. . . . Our job is to encourage them to become more self-sufficient."

Yet, other workers were less certain about the goals of welfare under welfare reform. For example, a front-line worker in Macomb County, Michigan, stated, "I don't really know anymore. It used to be providing aid to the indigent." Others clearly stated that determining eligibility for TANF was their chief priority. One worker from Hillsdale, Michigan, said that front-line staff spend a lot of time on paperwork to process applicants for benefit determination. She went on to say that

> Most of us rate how we do our job back to the [eligibility determination] stats. We don't have the time to spend worrying about what they [applicants and clients] are doing at Work First. If they get a job, it's nothing that we've done.

Asked what the goal of welfare is, a street-level worker in Detroit had this to say:

> To get the paperwork done. . . . But I think we all really believe that if we did our jobs, we'd work our way out of a job. That our job really is to get people to where they don't need us anymore.

Table 3.2. Front-Line Workers' Views on the Importance of Welfare Goals (percentages).

Workers' Views	To Agency	To State Officials	To Worker
Reducing the Number of People on Welfare	22.9	58.3	9.7
Determining Eligibility for Benefits and Services Accurately	22.3	10.7	22.7
Determining Eligibility in a Timely Manner	12.2	4.8	4.9
Diverting Applicants from Coming on Welfare	2.1	5.9	2.7
Requiring and Encouraging Work	4.3	4.3	7.0
Helping People Get the Best Possible Job They Can Get	3.2	0.5	4.9
Making Sure Everyone Who Is Eligible Receives Medical Benefits	2.1	1.1	2.7
Making Sure Everyone Who Is Eligible Receives Child Care	1.1	0.0	5.4
Helping People Achieve Self-Sufficiency	20.2	6.4	22.2
Preventing Fraudulent Behavior Among Clients	0.5	3.7	1.1
Reducing Out-of-Wedlock Births	1.1	2.7	2.2
Treating Clients Fairly and Equitably	8.0	1.6	14.6
	100.0	100.0	100.0

The survey data also reveal that despite management's declaration that "work first" is the primary goal of welfare, workers see *both* eligibility determination and welfare-to-work as the priorities. Survey questions for this research asked front-line workers on a Likert-type scale to indicate the importance of various welfare goals to themselves, to state officials (e.g., the governor; legislators), and to their agencies. Table 3.2 presents the results. As these data show, front-line workers overall tend to see their goals and their agencies' goals revolving around both determining eligibility ("accurately" and "in a timely manner") and the work-related goal of "helping people achieve self-sufficiency."[23] Other explicit work goals such as "requiring and encouraging work" and "helping people get the best possible job" were seen as less important to the workers and to their agencies.

Also, despite the welfare-to-work mandates promulgated by the states, the workers see the most important goal of welfare reform to state officials as getting people off welfare ("reducing the number of people on welfare"). A breakdown of the data by states (see table 3.3) further illustrates this point.

Table 3.3. Front-Line Workers' Views about the Importance of Welfare Goals, by State (percentages).

Texas	To Agency	To State Officials	To Worker
Reducing Number of People on Welfare	5.3	39.5	2.6
Determining Eligibility Accurately	21.1	13.2	39.5
Determining Eligibility in a Timely Manner	26.3	15.8	13.2
Diverting Applicants from Welfare	0.0	10.5	0.0
Requiring and Encouraging Work	2.6	2.6	7.9
Helping People Get the Best Possible Job	7.9	0.0	0.0
Making Sure Those Eligible Receive Med. Benefits	5.3	0.0	10.5
Making Sure Those Eligible Receive Child Care	0.0	0.0	0.0
Helping People Achieve Self-Sufficiency	26.3	7.9	15.8
Preventing Fraudulent Behavior Among Clients	0.0	7.9	0.0
Reducing Out-of-Wedlock Births	0.0	2.6	0.0
Treating Clients Fairly and Equitably	5.3	0.0	10.5

Georgia	To Agency	To State Officials	To Worker
Reducing Number of People on Welfare	17.8	48.6	6.8
Determining Eligibility Accurately	24.7	16.7	16.4
Determining Eligibility in a Timely Manner	8.2	2.8	4.1
Diverting Applicants from Welfare	4.1	9.7	4.1
Requiring and Encouraging Work	1.4	5.6	8.2
Helping People Get the Best Possible Job	2.7	1.4	8.2
Making Sure Those Eligible Receive Med. Benefits	1.4	1.4	0.0
Making Sure Those Eligible Receive Child Care	0.0	0.0	11.0
Helping People Achieve Self-Sufficiency	27.4	5.6	24.7
Preventing Fraudulent Behavior Among Clients	1.4	2.8	1.4
Reducing Out-of-Wedlock Births	2.7	4.2	4.1
Treating Clients Fairly and Equitably	8.2	1.4	11.0

These data suggest that public managers publicly state that the priority for their offices revolves around the new goals of welfare reform: moving clients into work and off of welfare. This is obviously an important message to convey publicly, and it certainly indicates that management officials are toeing the "official" line. But managers of local welfare offices further recognize the continued importance of the conflicting task of eligibility determination—their workers also

Table 3.3. (*continued*)

Michigan	To Agency	To State Officials	To Worker
Reducing Number of People on Welfare	39.5	75.7	11.1
Determining Eligibility Accurately	23.7	8.1	30.6
Determining Eligibility in a Timely Manner	18.4	2.7	2.8
Diverting Applicants from Welfare	0.0	0.0	2.8
Requiring and Encouraging Work	0.0	2.7	2.8
Helping People Get the Best Possible Job	2.6	0.0	5.6
Making Sure Those Eligible Receive Med. Benefits	2.6	2.7	2.8
Making Sure Those Eligible Receive Child Care	0.0	0.0	2.8
Helping People Achieve Self-Sufficiency	5.3	5.4	25.0
Preventing Fraudulent Behavior Among Clients	0.0	2.7	0.0
Reducing Out-of-Wedlock Births	0.0	0.0	0.0
Treating Clients Fairly and Equitably	7.9	0.0	13.9

New York	To Agency	To State Officials	To Worker
Reducing Number of People on Welfare	31.0	76.7	19.5
Determining Eligibility Accurately	19.0	2.3	14.6
Determining Eligibility in a Timely Manner	2.4	0.0	0.0
Diverting Applicants from Welfare	2.4	0.0	2.4
Requiring and Encouraging Work	14.3	4.7	7.3
Helping People Get the Best Possible Job	0.0	0.0	2.4
Making Sure Those Eligible Receive Med. Benefits	0.0	0.0	0.0
Making Sure Those Eligible Receive Child Care	4.8	0.0	2.4
Helping People Achieve Self-Sufficiency	14.3	7.0	22.0
Preventing Fraudulent Behavior Among Clients	0.0	2.3	2.4
Reducing Out-of-Wedlock Births	0.0	2.3	2.4
Treating Clients Fairly and Equitably	11.9	4.7	24.4

have a responsibility to deliver cash assistance effectively to those who qualify. Indeed, PRWORA recognizes this to be a critical task for welfare offices, even under welfare reform. As noted, PRWORA embraces the conflicting and dual goals of eligibility determination and welfare-to-work.[24] And, in fact, the states measure the performance of local offices not only by the percentage of TANF clients in a countable work activity (i.e., participation rates), but also by such eligibility determination measures as error rates (i.e., payment errors for

TANF) and standard of promptness (SOP). The SOP refers to the promptness with which applications and redeterminations for aid are processed. As of this writing, for example, in Georgia, applications for TANF must be acted upon by the DFCS within 45 days (performance issues are also discussed below).

An eligibility unit supervisor in Atlanta, Georgia, made the following remarks when asked specifically about the conflicting goals of welfare reform:

> It is to our advantage that some people still get TANF, because working counts as an activity if the worker is still on TANF. But if you get off welfare because you are making too much money, then we can't count you. So, the incentive is for the client not to get a good paying job. . . . Diversion is strived for because the incentive is to get people low-paying jobs, where they still qualify for TANF; we don't get rewarded for diverting clients. It's the placement rate that is looked at; 35% of our clients should be in an activity.

The job of managers in local welfare offices is a difficult and challenging one, to say the least. They must promote the priorities and goals articulated by state law and state officials. But, in accordance with PRWORA as well as with practical considerations, they must also ensure that the work of their offices—determining who is eligible for welfare assistance—continues to be performed in an efficient, effective, and fair manner. According to the street-level bureaucrats, local managers are conveying the importance of both goals.

Human Resources Management and Practices

As noted, local agency managers and supervisors are circumscribed with respect to their influence over certain personnel and human resources practices, as most of the rules and regulations are derived from state statutes and/or state constitutions. However, they are responsible for implementing a variety of personnel functions, which have the potential of influencing the practices of street-level welfare workers and, ultimately, organization outputs.

STAFF ORGANIZATION AND JOB CLASSIFICATION

Reclassifications of government jobs are generally designed and implemented at the state rather than the local level. Under welfare reform, a number of states reorganized staff or changed job classifications to conform with a case management approach, a holistic one where workers are responsible for managing and overseeing a case all the way from the point of in-take to employment. Unlike the more traditional eligibility-compliance approach, where caseworkers determine an applicant's eligibility for cash and other benefits and ensure client compliance with rules and requirements for the receipt of welfare, frontline workers under a case management approach provide more in-depth attention to family, including the services and benefits required by the family and assistance in finding the clients jobs. The intended purpose of this approach is to move away from welfare dependency to economic self-sufficiency.

In Michigan, caseworker positions were reclassified from income maintenance and JOBS workers—who determined eligibility, maintained cases for assistance programs and provided support services to welfare clients—to case management positions known as Family Independence Specialists (FIS or FISs). It was believed that this new role for caseworkers would help move TANF clients more readily into self-sufficiency. Instead of specialized roles, the FISs are expected to work more holistically with families, identifying barriers to employment, providing support services, and promoting independence and self-sufficiency. All nonfamily cases (e.g., exclusively food stamps or Medicaid cases) are processed by Eligibility Specialists. This cohort is not included in this study.

The other group of workers in the FIA that has some responsibility for processing TANF cases is the Registration Support Service (RSS). The RSS does the initial screening of TANF applicants.

In Georgia, job classifications were also changed to support a generic case management approach. More specialized personnel classifications were downgraded to create the new "generalist" position called Family Independence Case Manager (FICM), which combines the responsibilities formerly split among TANF, food stamp, Medicaid, and JOBS workers. Those case workers with FICM II classification are responsible for all job functions (i.e., TANF, food stamps, Medicaid, employment) for TANF clients, whereas those with FICM I classification are responsible only for employment services. It is important to note that grandparents who have responsibility for the children are not subject to job participation requirements or time limits.

In Texas, the Department of Human Services (DHS) has two categories of workers who have face-to-face interaction with TANF clients or applicants: receptionists and Texas Works Advisors (TWAs). The receptionists serve at the up-front stage of the TANF in-take process, collecting the application form and reviewing it for accuracy. The applicant is then referred to a TWA. Prior to welfare reform in Texas, the TWAs were referred to as eligibility specialists/in-take workers. While the job title has changed, the responsibilities have not. The TWAs are responsible for eligibility certification, client interviews, explaining benefits and requirements (work, Personal Responsibility Agreement, etc.), document verification, determining and redetermining benefits, work exemptions, and information and referral services.

In both Albany and Suffolk counties in New York, where welfare services are administered at the county level, no changes were made to the job classification system for DSS caseworkers. In both counties, job titles include, for example, eligibility, reception, and in-take.

Ultimately, however, it would seem that changes to job classification and staff organization had no demonstrable impact on the practices of front-line workers in welfare offices. While the changes may have made sense from a personnel standpoint, these reforms do little to encourage front-line staff in welfare offices to pursue the goal of moving welfare clients into jobs.

EMPLOYEE TRAINING

Management theory suggests that if an organization changes its mission or goals and expects its employees to perform the new tasks associated with those goals, the workers should be provided with some level of training. Survey questions asked all front-line workers whether

Table 3.4. Staff Self-Reporting on Training Received, by State (percentages).

Training Areas	Texas	Georgia	Michigan	New York
Financial Work Incentives	62.5	46.1	56.4	33.3
Temporary Deferrals/Exemptions	65.0	52.6	61.5	44.4
Transitional Benefits	72.5	63.2	53.8	42.2
Clients' Employability	32.5	56.6	28.2	48.9
Coaching/Counseling Clients on Work	52.5	47.4	59.0	33.3
Sanctioning	60.0	52.6	61.5	40.0
Improving Client's Self-Esteem	25.0	38.2	46.2	20.0
Monitoring Client's Work Participation	17.5	55.3	43.6	26.7
Reducing Error Rates in Eligibility/Benefits Determination	72.5	67.1	79.5	17.8
Removing Barriers to Employment	17.5	55.3	71.8	28.9
Verifying Client Information	67.5	61.8	30.8	28.9
Monitoring Clients' Time Limits	70.0	40.8	20.5	20.0
Granting Time Limit Extensions	47.5	18.4	7.7	17.8
Treating Clients Fairly and Equitably	80.0	75.0	48.7	60.0

they received training in specified areas, and, if they did, whether the training was formal, informal (e.g., via supervisors or coworkers; on-the-job-training), or a combination of both. Table 3.4 shows that front-line workers received training on a variety of topics, including eligibility determination under TANF as well as coaching and counseling clients about work and about their employability (note, however, the variation by state).

Table 3.5 shows whether the training was formal, informal, or both. Formal training would certainly tend to establish consistency and uniformity in the content of the training provided to all staff members. Moreover, it may ultimately be more effective, in that informal training, such as on-the-job training, occurs within the cultural context in which the new learning is applied, thus fostering the "old, familiar ways."[25] But, because of cost constraints, public agencies are often forced to rely on informal training, which leaves room for errors and inconsistencies in the instruction and information provided by the trainers. The data show that in New York and Michigan, training was

Table 3.5. Staff Self-Reporting on Type of Training, by State (percentages).

Training Areas	Texas			Georgia			Michigan			New York		
	Formal	Informal	Both	Formal	Informal	Both	Formal	Informal	Both	Formal	Informal	Both
Financial Work Incentives	32.5	20.0	7.5	11.8	15.8	50.0	30.8	15.4	43.6	22.2	6.7	66.7
Temporary Deferrals/Exemptions	30.0	22.5	7.5	27.6	11.8	18.4	10.3	43.6	5.1	38.0	51.0	23.0
Transitional Benefits	40.0	10.0	15.0	23.7	19.7	21.1	7.7	35.9	10.3	6.7	33.3	6.7
Clients' Employability	12.5	17.5	2.5	27.6	10.5	19.7	12.8	12.8	2.6	6.7	28.9	15.6
Coaching/Counseling Clients	17.5	15.0	17.5	19.7	10.5	21.1	33.3	12.8	10.3	6.7	17.8	11.1
Sanctioning	32.5	17.5	5.0	27.6	10.5	18.4	7.7	46.2	7.7	6.7	22.2	13.3
Improving Clients' Self-Esteem	2.5	7.5	7.5	10.5	18.4	13.2	25.6	10.3	10.3	15.6	2.2	4.4
Monitoring Clients' Work Participation	10.0	2.5	—	30.3	7.9	21.1	7.7	28.2	7.7	2.2	17.8	8.9
Reducing Error Rates in Eligibility/Benefits Determination	27.5	15.0	27.5	28.9	13.2	28.9	23.1	20.5	35.9	2.2	8.9	6.7
Removing Barriers to Employment	5.0	10.0	2.5	25.0	7.9	23.7	23.1	20.5	28.2	8.9	15.6	6.7
Verifying Client Information	25.0	15.0	17.5	14.5	17.1	32.9	5.1	23.1	2.6	4.4	17.8	8.9
Monitoring Clients' Time Limits	32.5	17.5	20.0	13.2	15.8	10.5	5.1	15.4	—	4.4	6.7	11.1
Granting Time Limit Extensions	30.0	12.5	5.0	9.2	3.9	10.5	—	5.1	2.6	2.2	8.9	8.9
Treating Clients Fairly and Equitably	34.4	15.6	50.0	34.4	18.0	47.5	26.3	26.3	47.4	18.5	37.0	44.4

Percentages may not total 100% due to missing values.

provided mostly on an informal and not a formal basis, while in Georgia and Texas, the reverse is true.

In some cases, managers or supervisors also received training. For example, in Michigan, managers received training on "Strength-Based Solutions" that stressed the notion that caseworkers can accomplish a lot if they focus on solutions and the client's strengths. Even managers admitted, however, that while this approach might make sense on a theoretical level, it is very difficult to put into practice. For example, one manager from a site in Michigan stated that "I thought it was a great theory but we don't have that kind of time, where you sit down and do an in-depth assessment. You hardly say anything. . . . We were used to getting information; trained in investigative interviewing like where did your income come from."

MONITORING AND EVALUATING JOB PERFORMANCE

As discussed earlier, the formal, stated goals of welfare have changed since the enactment of welfare reform across the nation. But a former goal also drives the welfare system: providing assistance to needy families so that children can remain with their parents or relatives. Thus, public managers are faced with a welfare system that embraces dual, conflicting goals.[26] In effect, PRWORA has resulted in ambiguities and complexities over performance standards for agencies and front-line workers.

The important public management question then arises: Against what performance standards are front-line workers measured? The information about performance can be useful for the organization in making decisions about pay, advancement, and discipline, but it is particularly useful in determining whether a formal incentive is created for front-line workers in welfare offices to pursue the goals of welfare reform as defined by their state and local welfare agencies.

Table 3.6 presents findings on the job tasks for which front-line staff report they are monitored. An interesting finding is that in every state, a high percentage of front-line staff report that they are monitored on eligibility functions or tasks. For example, high percentages of workers in all states except New York report that they are monitored on such

Table 3.6. Formal Monitoring of Job Tasks, according to Front-Line Staff in Welfare Offices, by State (percentages).

Job Tasks	Texas		Georgia	
	No	Yes	No	Yes
Reducing People on Welfare	50.0	7.5	30.6	33.3
Determining Eligibility Accurately	7.7	76.9	2.6	77.6
Determining Eligibility in Timely Manner	5.1	74.4	1.3	76.3
Diverting Applicants from Welfare	50.0	12.5	40.0	21.3
Requiring and Encouraging Work	75.0	12.5	50.0	32.9
Helping People Get the Best Job	35.9	2.6	40.8	13.2
Ensuring Those Eligible for Medical Benefits Receive Them	25.6	59.0	23.7	43.4
Ensuring Those Eligible for Child Care Receive It	21.6	10.8	28.9	44.7
Helping People Achieve Self-Sufficiency	52.6	10.5	40.8	34.2
Preventing Fraud	22.5	50.0	32.4	43.2
Reducing Out-of-Wedlock Births	15.0	0.0	25.0	6.6
Treating Clients Fairly and Equitably	20.0	77.5	24.0	68.0

Job Tasks	Michigan		New York	
	No	Yes	No	Yes
Reducing People on Welfare	25.6	69.2	28.9	31.1
Determining Eligibility Accurately	25.6	71.8	31.1	33.3
Determining Eligibility in Timely Manner	5.1	92.3	22.2	37.8
Diverting Applicants from Welfare	60.5	2.6	26.7	17.8
Requiring and Encouraging Work	57.9	36.8	40.0	28.9
Helping People Get the Best Job	61.5	0.0	24.4	11.1
Ensuring Those Eligible for Medical Benefits Receive Them	55.3	36.8	22.2	37.8
Ensuring Those Eligible for Child Care Receive It	68.4	26.3	31.1	28.9
Helping People Achieve Self-Sufficiency	73.7	18.4	33.3	24.4
Preventing Fraud	81.6	5.3	42.2	20.0
Reducing Out-of-Wedlock Births	34.2	0.0	2.2	2.2
Treating Clients Fairly and Equitably	76.3	23.7	51.1	42.2

Percentages may not total 100% because of missing values.

Note: "No" indicates where staff performance is either not monitored or only informally monitored.

functions as "determining eligibility accurately" and "determining eligibility in a timely manner," goals that were viewed as being important to the workers and to their agencies (these are the performance measures—error rates and the SOP—discussed earlier). Even in New York, the percentage of workers responding that they are formally monitored on these eligibility functions is relatively high compared with other tasks.

Another interesting finding as seen in table 3.6 is that in every state a relatively high percentage of front-line workers report that they are *not* monitored on "requiring and encouraging work" or "helping people achieve self-sufficiency." It may be recalled that this latter work-related task of helping clients achieve self-sufficiency was viewed as an important goal to workers and their agencies. But, as noted earlier, the task of helping clients find jobs does not fall within the purview of front-line workers in welfare agencies. It is the task of workers in the employment offices to fulfill this goal.

It would appear, then, that managers in local welfare offices are evaluating workers predominately on eligibility determination functions, which are most critical to welfare offices, but not on any of the tasks related to welfare-to-work goals, which are more critical to the employment agencies.

MANAGEMENT AND LEADERSHIP STYLES

The survey asked front-line workers to rate a number of dimensions associated with effective management and leadership. For example, as reported in table 3.7, front-line workers were asked whether staff meetings were held regularly. In Texas, 95 percent of the workers responded "yes"; in Michigan, 90 percent said yes; in Georgia, 80 percent said yes; and in New York, not even half of the workers (43 percent) said yes.

Survey results for workers' responses to other aspects of effective leadership and management are also presented in table 3.7. As the data show, front-line workers in every state have very positive views about the management and leadership styles exhibited by their supervisors. In particular, workers see a very open style of communication between

Table 3.7. Front-Line Workers' Views of Management and Leadership Practices in Local Welfare Offices.

Workers' Views	Texas		Georgia	
	Mean	S.D.	Mean	S.D.
Workers' Freedom to Raise Issues	3.7	1.2	3.8	1.3
Overall Job Satisfaction	3.5	1.0	3.3	1.2
Decision-Making Structure	2.2	1.3	2.4	1.3
Open Communication with Supervisor	4.2	1.0	4.5	0.9
Lateral Communication	4.3	0.9	4.4	1.0
Downward Communication	4.0	1.0	3.7	1.0
Supervisor Loyalty to Staff	3.9	1.2	4.1	1.2
Supervisor Creativity	3.8	1.0	3.9	1.2
	$n = 40$		$n = 76$	
Meetings Scheduled Regularly?	95% said yes		80% said yes	

Workers' Views	Michigan		New York	
	Mean	S.D.	Mean	S.D.
Workers' Freedom to Raise Issues	4.2	1.1	3.6	1.3
Overall Job Satisfaction	2.8	1.3	3.0	1.2
Decision-Making Structure	2.3	1.2	2.6	1.3
Open Communication with Supervisor	4.3	1.1	4.5	0.9
Lateral Communication	4.6	0.7	4.3	0.9
Downward Communication	3.1	1.1	3.3	1.3
Supervisor Loyalty to Staff	3.9	1.4	4.0	1.2
Supervisor Creativity	3.8	1.2	3.9	1.1
	$n = 39$		$n = 43$	
Meetings Scheduled Regularly?	90% said yes		43% said yes	

Scale: 1 to 5, where 1 is low and 5 is high.

themselves and their supervisors, with very good lateral communication. Downward communication, on the other hand, varied by state. This particular question asked, "How good is the communication of information downward (from office managers to supervisors to you)?"

Front-line workers also perceive a high degree of loyalty shown to them by their supervisors; they also find their supervisors to be creative and innovative. Interestingly, despite these very positive perceptions overall, front-line workers in every state see the decision-making structures in their offices as "very hierarchical" and very centralized, "where the decisions are made only by supervisors and the higher-ups."

Finally, the overall job satisfaction of front-line workers ranged from 2.8 in Michigan to 3.5 in Texas. The question was calibrated as follows:

1 = Not at All Satisfied

3 = Neutral

5 = Very Satisfied

Summary

As seen in this chapter, the role of public managers in welfare offices, as in other public agencies, is a difficult and challenging one. Faced with ambiguous goals and policy mandates, as well as conflicting performance standards, public managers must carefully balance the need to fulfill state-level mandates to move people off welfare and into jobs with efforts to ensure that welfare clients are processed for eligibility of benefits in an efficient, fair manner. Moreover, public managers are faced with various additional constraints that circumscribe their ability to manage front-line workers. Civil service rules, shrinking budgets (e.g., for training), and conflicting performance measures to evaluate staff limit managerial capacity, ultimately creating an environment which makes managing both an "art" and a "science."[27]

Despite these constraints, managers and supervisors have developed ways to affect organization outputs: moving the work of their staff and their agencies forward, that is to say, ensuring that welfare services and benefits are delivered to the clients. Although managers publicly state that "work first" is the main priority, they have successfully sent the signal to workers that eligibility determination and self-sufficiency are both goals to be striven for. Both are called for under the welfare reform law. Yet managers do not hold their workers to performance standards that are state-driven, and that are *not* within the purview of their workers—finding jobs for clients to help them achieve self-sufficiency. Managers and supervisors in local welfare offices instead continue to measure the performance of workers on criteria associated with their workers' job requirements—effectively determining eligibility for benefits. Here, error rates and standard of promptness (SOP) are the critical performance measures.

The workers themselves revealed that there is conflict around the goals of welfare: in the survey data as well as in the face-to-face interviews, staff sometimes echoed the mantra of "welfare-to-work." Others continue to see getting the paperwork done (for eligibility determination) as being most important. In fact, workers consistently stated that implementing the plethora of new rules for eligibility determination has created so much paperwork that there is little time to do anything else. There were also workers who expressed uncertainty about what their jobs actually entailed under welfare reform. The issue of conflicting priorities and goals in local welfare offices is important because it creates opportunities for managers to redirect the behaviors of their workers. This issue will be addressed further in chapter 5.

We also saw that managers and supervisors have ensured that workers receive some training on both new eligibility determination requirements under TANF and coaching clients about self-sufficiency (i.e., finding jobs, even though welfare workers are not responsible for doing so). In addition, management skills and practices are viewed very positively by the workers, which is very important for a healthy, productive work environment. Thus, it would appear that management does matter at the broad, macro level of policy reform, and also at the local level of government in terms of organization outputs.

But the question still remains, does public management affect the actual practices and activities of street-level bureaucrats? Or do other factors, such as worker norms and culture, have a greater influence on the work of street-level bureaucrats? The following chapter seeks to answer some of these questions.

CHAPTER FOUR

Public Management and Street-Level Bureaucrats

There is a long tradition of research in the social sciences on the multiple interests that interact to influence and shape policies as they devolve down hierarchical lines.[1] The sequence of decisions by which laws become administrative rules, then programs, and ultimately front-line service delivery practices illustrates the management and politics of policymaking in a very fundamental way. It is axiomatic that politics permeates the adoption of law. A host of elected, appointed, and career officials, whose interests are not necessarily consonant, come together to interpret the law, issue rules and regulations, and carry them out. Local agency officials, also with their own sets of interests, subsequently try to make sense of these directives by developing and implementing programs and policies for their clients. Street-level workers then bring yet another and often different set of interests to the process, which further affects policy delivery and outputs.

This chapter examines the impact of management in terms of administrative capacity (e.g., human resources practices) and managerial behaviors (e.g., management styles) in local welfare offices on the actual behaviors of front-line workers in terms of service delivery. It begins with a review of the literature on street-level bureaucratic behavior and the various factors, including management, that influence the behaviors of street-level workers. Referring back to the model presented in chapter 1, it then examines whether and how management affects the behaviors of street-level bureaucrats under welfare reform.

The Power of Street-Level Bureaucrats

Elmore has referred to the traditional top–down, hierarchical approach to policy implementation as "forward mapping." He also refers to another critical approach to policy implementation as "backward mapping."[2] It occurs at the lowest level of implementation, where actions or specific behaviors are discretionary.[3] The level referred to here is the street level of bureaucracy, where front–line workers bring their interests to the process to further affect policy delivery and output. There is in fact a rich body of literature on the critical role that street–level bureaucrats play in the implementation of public policy.[4]

A pioneer of research on street-level bureaucracy, Lipsky illustrated that front-line workers have a good deal of discretionary power, which ultimately enables them to effect policy implementation at the street level of bureaucracy. As he explains:

> Street-level bureaucrats make policy in two related respects. They exercise wide discretion in decisions about citizens with whom they interact. Then, when taken in concert, their individual actions add up to agency behavior.[5]

Similarly, Maynard-Moody and Musheno point out that discretion is inevitable at the street level of bureaucracy. They go on to say that despite the fact that rules permeate the jobs of street-level workers, discretion prevails. Maynard-Moody and Musheno state that

> every aspect of street-level work is defined by rules and procedures . . . yet rules and procedures provide only weak constraints on the loose parameters around street-level judgments. Street-level work is, ironically, rule saturated, not rule bound.[6]

Maynard-Moody and Musheno reiterate this in a more recent work, *Cops, Teachers, Counselors: Stories from the Front Lines of Public Service.* They point out that

> street-level workers must decide which rules or procedures to apply. The proliferation of rules—often contradictory rules—requires matching the case to the rule or procedure, and this process requires discre-

tion. . . . Thus, like putty, discretion can be squeezed by oversight and rules but never eliminated; it will shift and reemerge in some other form in some other place. This is a fact of life in the modern state.[7]

Many have pointed to the particular salience of street-level bureaucracy in the human services, despite the fact that it is very rule-driven.[8] Hasenfeld points out, for example, that the impact of street-level bureaucrats working within the human services is quite appreciable because they "process people."[9] Along the same lines, Scott points out that although rules and regulations somewhat circumscribe the behaviors of street-level bureaucrats, workers are responsible for translating persons into clients. He argues that street-level bureaucrats are

> responsible for translating clients into bureaucratically defined categories in order to provide services, treatment, and other forms of assistance. . . . Street-level bureaucrats use this discretion to manipulate the information about its clients that is available to the organization and to limit the agency's ability to influence their own behaviors.[10]

In addition, Keiser notes that bureaucrats at the front lines of social services agencies wield a good deal of policymaking power because they determine which citizens will receive welfare benefits and which will not.[11] She goes on to say that:

> Because of this, the caseworkers who interact directly with clients . . . play an especially important role in determining how benefits are distributed. Street-level bureaucrats must transform citizens into clients— take individuals and place them in administrative categories such as "mentally ill," "alcoholic," or "poor" (Prottas 1979). In doing so, street-level bureaucrats act as the gatekeepers into welfare programs. Because many social welfare programs rely on administrative categories that are subjective, street-level bureaucrats have discretion in how social welfare programs are administered.[12]

The street-level workers included in this study certainly exhibited discretionary power. In fact, in one encounter in Dallas, Texas, a front-

line worker was specifically asked why she made a particular determination to approve benefits for the applicant, and she stated: "Well,
maybe 'cause it's a man; we rarely get men in here. It's also extenuat-
ing circumstances—he has a child and no money."

In an almost ironic use of discretion, one street-level worker tried
to persuade an applicant to apply for TANF. This is an excerpt from an
encounter at a Dallas, Texas, welfare office:

WORKER: So, I see you want emergency food stamps and AFDC?
   [*doesn't use the new term, TANF*]
APPLICANT: I changed my mind. I don't want AFDC.
WORKER: What do you mean, you changed your mind? Why don't you
   want AFDC?
APPLICANT: I just don't want it. I made a mistake when I checked that
   box off.
WORKER: You know that TANF is a way for you to get a job and I see
   it's been a long time since you've worked. TANF will help you find
   a job and to go back to work. You would have more to prove to
   get some money, but with your daughter, who is not yet three, you
   could get $163 a month. Also, TANF will also help with training
   opportunities and we could help you find child care.
APPLICANT: I am not interested.
WORKER: So you are declining assistance under TANF?
APPLICANT: Yes.
WORKER: What about Medicaid? You can apply for Medicaid without
   applying for TANF, and you have a young child. Do you want to
   apply for Medicaid?
APPLICANT: No.

The applicant was eventually approved for food stamps.

In short, while there are many actors in the welfare reform policy
process, it is the street-level workers that may have the greatest influence on the outcomes of social programs or policies.[13] And these outcomes can sometimes differ from the policies advanced or articulated
by state policy- and lawmakers. Given street-level bureaucrats'

considerable sphere of influence over the delivery of public policies and programs, a very compelling question has yet to be answered: Does management have some control over the behaviors and actions of front-line workers in their delivery of public services?

The Role of Management in Street-Level Bureaucratic Behavior

There are a number of studies that have examined the potential determinants of bureaucratic behavior.[14] For example, Scott looks at the impact of such factors as organizational characteristics (e.g., degree of formalization), worker compassion toward clients, and individual decision-maker characteristics (e.g., education and gender) on the awarding of welfare benefits to clients. He finds that organizational factors such as formalization and worker compassion toward welfare clients had the strongest influence on bureaucrats' propensity to award clients benefits and services. He also found professionalism to be important. Individual decision-maker attributes were found to have no impact on the behavior of street-level bureaucrats.[15]

Others have examined similar organizational and individual-level characteristics (e.g., professional norms and culture, race, education, community and personal values) as potential determinants of bureaucratic behavior.[16] As much of this research shows, one of the most salient factors influencing street-level bureaucratic behavior is professional norms.

Existing research, however, has a few lacunae, the most important being the potential impact of public managers on the behaviors or actions of street-level bureaucrats. While existing research has not looked specifically at the role of managers and leaders, at least one study considers the role of public management from the standpoint of managerial or administrative capacity in front-line service delivery. Jodi Sandfort, in her ethnographic case study, examines the potential influence of the new public management and traditional public administrative practices on front-line action in two local welfare offices and two private Work First or employment contractors in Michigan. She concludes that neither performance-based management nor traditional bureaucratic directives have an impact on front-line practices in either type of agency.[17] She finds, instead, that the more powerful determinants of street-level behavior rest in the collective beliefs or "schemas" of front-line staff (e.g., collective beliefs, norms, shared knowledge of the organizational members) as well as the "resources" (e.g., workers' reliance on concrete tools such as job search videos) available to them.

Sandfort's finding that work norms, shared knowledge, and socialization help define work behaviors at the front lines of service delivery is an important one. In fact, it is interesting to note that Mary Parker Follett and Chester Barnard called for studying the social aspects of organizations in their pioneering work on formal and "informal" organization. Sandfort's and others' findings here lend support for Follett and Barnards's proposition that characteristics of "informal" organization such as professionalism and socialization are significant determinants of how agencies operate.[18]

Sandfort's research is certainly critical, but as she acknowledges, she does not account for the potential impact of "local managers or familiar management infrastructures."[19] Rather, as Scott and others did, Sandfort looks at the *attributes* of bureaucracies themselves, such as "minute regulations," "policy manuals" and "standardized forms." Thus, her conclusions actually suggest that *not* management per se but formal bureaucratic structure, as defined by rules and regulations, has little impact on the behaviors of front-line workers. This in itself is a significant finding, supporting previous research that the power of street-level workers, despite operating in rule-driven bureaucracies, is considerable.[20]

Does Management Matter at the Street-Level of Bureaucracy?

One important question that has yet to be answered is, what impact does management have on the behaviors of street-level bureaucrats?

More specifically, are management practices associated with encouraging street-level bureaucrats to pursue the new welfare goals, either those expressed formally (welfare-to-work) or informally (diversion or deterrence)? Or, based on the discussion in chapter 3, are managers leading front-line staff to pursue other goals, such as determining eligibility in an efficient, effective manner?

These three goal clusters—(1) "eligibility determination," (2) "employment," and (3) "diversion"—serve as the dependent variables for the empirical examination of this question.[21] Goals in the "eligibility determination" index relate to the more traditional goals of the welfare system: the timely and accurate processing of welfare claims. Goals in the "employment" index relate to new welfare reform goals requiring and supporting employment. Those in the "diversion" index relate to a variety of federal and local goals to deter welfare use, prevent fraudulent claims, and discourage out-of-wedlock births.

The research asks, "To what degree do local management capacity, practices, and characteristics explain variation in street-level bureaucratic behavior around these goal indices?"

As described more fully in chapter 1 and appendix B, the direct observations or encounters provide data on the actual content and process of front-line practices in welfare offices. A total of 730 encounters in welfare offices are included in this study. A brief analysis of these encounters indicates that street-level bureaucrats discussed eligibility determination more than the other topics. Table 4.1 provides data on the frequency with which the topic clusters were discussed in the encounters. As the data show, eligibility determination activities for TANF occurred, or were a topic of discussion, in 50.1 percent of the encounters. Employment issues were discussed in 33.1 percent of the encounters, and diversion in 15.9 percent. The data further show that the average number of times eligibility determination activities occurred or were the topic of discussion per encounter was 6.5, as compared to 4.2 for employment and 2 for diversion. However, as indicated by the relatively large standard deviations, there is a high degree of variance in the number of times each topic was addressed or mentioned per encounter.

Table 4.1. Frequency with Which Topics Were Discussed or Occurred in Welfare Departments, All States.

Topic	Topic of Discussion (%)	Range of Occurrences per Encounter	Mean	S.D.
Eligibility Determination	50.1	0–47	6.5	6.8
Employment	33.1	0–43	4.2	5.5
Diversion	15.9	0–17	2.0	2.9

$n = 730$ encounters.

Factors That Can Impact Street-Level Behavior

Several measures are relied upon for the independent variables of primary interest: administrative capacity and management behaviors and practices, as addressed more fully in chapters 1 and 3 (see also figure 1.3 for an illustration of the model for this research). Management behaviors and practices refer to such factors as communication and decision-making styles or practices. For example, one measure of management behavior is the degree to which managers allow for employee participation in decision making. Based on survey questions, the degree to which staff perceive a participatory style of management was measured on a scale from 1 to 5, where 1 = "centralized" and 5 = "decentralized." The survey stated that "decentralized" means "where front-line workers such as yourself participate in various types of decisions."

Another measure of management practice captures the general communication style of supervisors. This variable was constructed by summing staff responses to questions about the openness of communication with their supervisor as well as the overall quality of communication.

In addition to management and leadership behaviors or practices, administrative capacity is also expected to affect the behavior of front-line workers. Administrative or managerial capacity refers to such factors as human resources practices—this includes, for example, performance monitoring and the extent of training provided to front-line workers around the new welfare-to-work goals. While managers at the local level have little control over the formal resources allocated for any type of training, this variable will indicate whether managers and supervisors made some provisions for training (e.g., on-the-job training by supervisors and/or the workers themselves).

As discussed in chapter 3, the survey instrument included a six-item index to measure staff perceptions on the extent to which they had received training on topics specifically related to the new employment-related goals (training on explaining financial incentives for working, explaining transitional benefits for those leaving welfare for work, assessing client employability, coaching and counseling clients about work, monitoring work behaviors, and removing employment barriers). Staff rated their training during the prior three years on a three-point scale from 1 = "none" to 3 = "both formal and informal" training. Variables on training in each of the three areas—eligibility determination, employment, diversion—are included in the models.

Another administrative capacity or human resources management factor examined in this study revolves around the tasks on which workers' performance is monitored (e.g., eligibility determination, employment, or diversion). Importantly, local welfare managers are hamstrung with respect to performance indicators, which are generally set by state civil service laws or their administering bodies. Moreover, as Lipsky observes, "Street-level bureaucrats characteristically work in jobs with conflicting and ambiguous goals." He goes on to ask: "Are the goals of public welfare to provide income support or decrease dependence?"[22] In effect, performance management for government workers becomes quite challenging. Do managers measure workers' performance against the goals of eligibility determination, diversion, or finding jobs for welfare recipients?

To account for these systemic inconsistencies, survey questions captured the extent to which staff perceive they are being monitored not on "actual" agency goals, but on *their perceptions of* their agencies' goals. Staff were asked to rate how their performance was monitored on tasks relating to the three goal indices, with the scale set up as: 0 = "not part of my job," 1 = "not monitored or monitored informally," or 2 "monitored and/or tracked formally." Variables on supervision and monitoring around each individual goal cluster are included in the models.

There are a number of other factors supported by the existing research, as noted above, which can affect the behavior of street-level bureaucrats. As Meyers and Vorsanger point out,

> The capacity of any single factor to influence [workers'] discretionary behavior—whether the factor is a policy officials' directive or a local agency's culture—is mediated by the influence of other, oftentimes competing forces in the implementation system.[23]

Organization factors such as how welfare services are administered—state, county, or both—are considered a potential predictor of street-level bureaucratic behavior. As noted, for the states included in this study, Michigan and Texas represent state-administered systems, New York is county-administered and Georgia represents a mixture of both state- and county-administered. Thus, "service mix" is included as an independent variable.[24]

Another potential variable that can impact the actions of front-line workers is compassion or altruism, as Scott described. His research, as discussed earlier, found worker compassion toward clients to be a strong predictor of street-level bureaucratic behavior.[25] Survey questions asked workers their opinions about welfare clients, such as whether it is difficult to get off of welfare and if clients are on welfare due to circumstances beyond their control.

Some scholars have found that the behaviors of street-level bureaucrats are affected not so much by organizational or policy directives, but rather by professional interests and norms. As noted earlier, Sandfort has made a significant contribution to the literature on street-level bureaucracy. She found that "schemas" have a salient impact on the behavior of front-line staff. As she illustrates, work norms and shared knowledge and beliefs about work routines and outcomes become part of the organization's culture, which ultimately drives the work of street-level bureaucrats.[26]

Similarly, Brehm and Gates find that formal policy directives have very little control over the behaviors of bureaucrats at the front lines of service delivery, especially in social services and policing, because they are largely self-regulated. They conclude that bureaucrats behave in certain ways because they embrace the norms of public service and these norms are shared and reinforced by their coworkers.[27]

Meyers and Vorsanger, in their review of the literature on street-level bureaucrats, suggest that worker ideology is extremely "consequential for discretionary behaviors, from their socialization into professional norms to their personal beliefs about policy instruments and targets."[28]

Lipsky points out that "The work environment of street-level bureaucrats is structured by common conditions that give rise to common patterns of practice and affect the direction these patterns take."[29] As they amass time on the job, workers socialize into and, in fact, internalize the culture of the organization, which consciously or unconsciously guides their day-to-day activities. And the more time on the job, the more a worker knows and internalizes the "ropes" of the job. For the sample included in this study, front-line staff worked an average of ten years with welfare clients; their experience dealing with clients ranged from a few months to thirty-six years. A variable measuring the amount of time front-line staff have worked with welfare clients is included and serves as a proxy for work norms, shared knowledge, and socialization.

Drawing on prior organizational theory and research, various characteristics of individual decision makers may also impact the behavior of street-level bureaucrats. One factor, as many have pointed out, is education, which has been typically measured by degree attainment. Education not only reflects a sense of professionalism but it can also reflect and relate to shared knowledge and beliefs, which Sandfort sees as part of work norms and culture.[30] It represents how workers may perform their jobs, and in this sense it characterizes a work ethic. Education, then, is included as an independent variable in the models, representing not just professionalism but also occupational culture. It is important to note that even if welfare workers are not formally educated beyond high school, the workers are socialized into the job, and hence the culture of the occupation or "profession." As discussed, length of time on the job can also capture work norms and culture.

In addition, as many have suggested, the gender and race of the worker can affect front-line behavior in welfare offices.[31] These independent variables are also included in the models.

Table 4.2. Front-Line Workers by Gender.

Gender	No.	%
Women	204	80.6
Men	49	19.4
Totals	253	100.0

There were 33 cases of missing data on gender.

Findings

Tables 4.2, 4.3, and 4.4 present descriptive statistics on a number of variables of interest. Table 4.2 shows that about 80 percent of the front-line workers in the sample are women, and, as seen in table 4.3, 52 percent of the workers are white, with 40 percent being African American, 4.3 percent Latino, 0.5 percent Asian, and 3.1 percent listed as other (e.g., Middle Eastern). In addition, table 4.5 presents a breakdown of workers by educational status. As the data indicate, 31 percent of the front-line workers have a bachelor's degree, and 27.4 percent have some college credits. About 13 percent have some graduate work or a master's degree or higher, and 11.2 percent have a high school diploma only.

Table 4.5 presents the results of the ordinary least squares (OLS) regression analyses estimating the contribution of management, leadership, organizational structure, culture, and other factors on the behaviors of street-level bureaucrats in welfare offices. Interestingly, the management, leadership, and organizational variables have no significant impact on the behaviors and actions of street-level bureaucrats in any of the three goal clusters. Rather, variables representing professional

Table 4.3. Front-Line Workers by Ethnicity.

Ethnicity	No.	%
White (not Hispanic)	98	52.1
African American (not Hispanic)	75	40.0
Latino/Hispanic (regardless of race)	8	4.3
Asian or Pacific Islander	1	0.5
Other	6	3.1
Totals	188	100.0

There were several pieces of missing data on ethnicity.

Table 4.4. Front-Line Workers, Educational Attainment.

Educational Attainment	No.	%
GED	1	0.5
High School Diploma	22	11.2
Some College	54	27.4
Associate's Degree	32	16.2
Bachelor's Degree	62	31.3
Some Graduate Work	15	7.6
Master's Degree or Higher	11	5.6
Totals	197	100.0

There are missing data on educational attainment.

norms and culture seem to be more important to street-level bureaucratic behavior. And these variables are important for eligibility determination behaviors.[32]

The data show that such factors as education and years working with welfare clients, proxies for culture and professional norms, have a positive effect on street-level behavior revolving around eligibility determination. So, too, does worker compassion, which can also develop over time, and can lead to workers providing more benefits to clients.[33]

Importantly, the findings here support propositions that factors such as professional norms, culture, and socialization are strong predictors of work behaviors. This is a significant finding, because it suggests that managers and leaders are less able to manage and impact the actual work of their staff. As noted earlier, Sandfort and others have argued that collectively held beliefs and shared knowledge shape workers' behaviors.[34] These abstract beliefs find expression in special language, actions, taboos, and "rituals" that characterize what workers do, how they do it, and how they socialize within the workplace.[35]

In addition, as noted already, Maynard-Moody and Musheno found in their critical study of street-level workers that while "policies, rules, and administrative oversight pervade their work and are ever present in their calculations about what to do," workers' behaviors are influenced more by their own moral judgments, which are based on their personal knowledge of and constant interactions with clients. The voices of street-level workers, as they note, "convey a strong orienta-

Table 4.5. Management and Street-Level Bureaucratic Behavior (OLS Multiple Regression).

Behavior	Eligibility Determination	Employment	Diversion
	Beta	Beta	Beta
Supervision/Monitoring	−0.05	0.09	0.06
Training	0.02	0.05	−0.11
Decision-Making Structure	0.03	0.10	0.08
Open Communication	−0.12	0.04	0.02
Gender of Worker	0.07	0.02	0.13
Ethnicity of Worker	−0.03	−0.10	−0.01
Education	0.2***	0.14	0.14
Years Working with Welfare Clients	0.15**	0.10	0.07
Compassion for Welfare Clients	0.19***	0.08	0.07
Service Mix	0.17**	0.14*	−0.07
R^2	0.20	0.16	0.07
Adjusted R^2	0.14	0.09	0.01

* $p < .10$
** $p < .05$
*** $p < .01$

tion . . . toward the workers' own beliefs, their value systems, in explaining their decision making."[36]

It is also significant that the professional norms and occupational culture variables matter for worker behavior around eligibility determination, and *not* the explicit goals of welfare reform (i.e., welfare-to-work) or the implicit goals (i.e., diversion or deterrence). Efforts to bring about major change to any organizational system or scheme may impel workers to find safety and security in the traditional routines of their jobs (here, eligibility determination). In addition, workers also recognize collectively that despite efforts to change the goals of the welfare system, they are still responsible for determining whether people qualify to receive welfare benefits. And, as managers and supervisors have conveyed (see chapter 3), workers' performance continues to be measured against eligibility determination criteria such as standard of promptness and error rates. Thus, the workers will find it desirable—perhaps even necessary—to continue to focus on eligibility determination functions as opposed to employment or diversion.

Finally, it is worth noting that the one other variable that shows some significance for worker behavior around eligibility determination as well as employment is service mix. The positive coefficients suggest that these types of behaviors are more prevalent in states where services are administered not at the state but at the county level (i.e., New York) or at both the county and state levels (i.e., Georgia).

Management and Job Satisfaction

Although the results presented above suggest that management may not have an impact on the actions or behavior of street-level bureaucrats, management factors can influence the job satisfaction of welfare workers.[37] Social service occupations, because of the nature of the clientele, can be extremely challenging and stressful. As such, job satisfaction is a crucial ingredient to the work environment. As human resource specialists have long emphasized, job satisfaction may not motivate employees to do what their supervisors want them to do, but it does prevent employees from being *dissatisfied* with their jobs, and hence poor performers.[38]

In addition, a myriad of research has shown that job satisfaction leads to greater overall organizational productivity.[39] As Wexley and Yukl point out, job satisfaction affects "organizational effectiveness to the extent that [it influences] turnover, absenteeism, strikes, grievances, sabotage, theft, and so on." They go on to say that satisfied employees make better employees, for which reason, "job satisfaction is one of the most popular indicators used by consultants and researchers for assessing organizational effectiveness."[40]

Table 4.6 presents the OLS multiple regression analysis results for the effects of management factors on the job satisfaction of street-level bureaucrats in welfare agencies. As the data show, open communications, participatory management, and high worker morale are positively correlated with worker job satisfaction. Again, job satisfaction is a necessary component to the workplace, helping to improve organizational effectiveness and also preventing workers from becoming dissatisfied with their jobs.

Table 4.6. Management and Job Satisfaction of Street-Level Bureaucrats (OLS Multiple Regression, Standardized Coefficients).

Management	Beta	SE
Decision–Making Structure	0.06	0.06
Open Communication	0.15★★★	0.07
Worker Morale	0.44★★★	0.06
Participatory Management	0.13★★	0.06
R²	0.34	
Adjusted R²	0.33	

★ p<.10
★★ p<.05
★★★ p<.01
Dependent variable is job satisfaction of front-line workers.

What Matters at the Street Level?

There is an abundance of evidence that management does make a difference in the operations and productivity of public sector bureaucracies. Earlier chapters provide evidence to this effect. However, the one level of bureaucratic activity in the public sector where management may have less of an impact is at the street level. The reason for this may hinge on the work culture, professional norms, and "schemas" that imbue professional life in bureaucracies, especially at the front lines of service delivery.

The research presented in this chapter supports this phenomenon. First, despite the formal and informal goals of welfare reform (i.e., welfare-to-work and diversion, respectively), front-line staff continue to engage in eligibility determination activities. Second, it is the work ethics, norms, professionalism, and occupational culture at the street level of bureaucracy that influence the behaviors of front-line staff, *not* management, leadership, and organizational factors. Third, this finding notwithstanding, workers are doing what local managers expect of them—eligibility determination. As we saw in chapter 3, front-line staff continue to be measured against such eligibility determination criteria as error rates and standard of promptness. This sends an important signal to workers about what is expected of them. It must also be kept in mind that welfare reform created an extraordinary quantity of new rules and regulations that workers must follow. Moreover, with new rules and regulations comes paperwork. Thus, determining eligibility in an efficient, effective manner is still a key task for the welfare bureaucracy.

But while front-line workers may be doing what managers at the local levels of bureaucracy expect of them, the workers *are not* doing what the elected officials—in particular, governors and state legislatures—and high-level bureaucrats expected them to do. That is to say, street-level bureaucrats are not implementing the policies that the "state" intended to be delivered. Again, this is not necessarily an explicit attempt by bureaucrats to sabotage the operations of the bureaucracy. Nevertheless, it raises the paramount question, how can the state control the bureaucracy if the bureaucrats can't be controlled? As noted in chapter 1, there is large body of literature showing that bureaucracies, given their very entrenched nature, cannot be readily changed or redirected; they are virtually impenetrable.[41] The current research supports this premise. Although it is beyond the scope of this study, this has implications, in a broader sense, for democracy and the relationship between the citizen and the state—that which the state expects to be delivered to citizens is not actually being delivered.

In the context of welfare reform, perhaps the state in fact recognized that it could not control the behaviors of bureaucrats in its efforts to redirect the activities of an entrenched, immutable welfare bureaucracy, which for decades has been mired in an eligibility-compliance culture. This may be precisely why states made the conscious decision to place the responsibility for the delivery of employment services into an organizational unit separate from the income maintenance delivery unit. If it is virtually impossible to redirect the activities of the welfare bureaucracy, then why not create a new bureaucracy to perform the desired tasks, or engage the aid of an existing bureaucracy already performing the desired function (in this case, departments of labor delivering employment services) to implement the new policy—moving people off welfare and into jobs? And, from the state's perspective, whether or not welfare recipients are actually able to find well-paying jobs, at least they are moved off of welfare. The decision to separate welfare or income maintenance services from employment or welfare-to-work services is a compelling explanation for how the welfare system was reformed.

CHAPTER FIVE

The Art and Science of Managing Street-Level Bureaucrats

In the previous chapter, we learned that front-line staff rely heavily on professional experience, work norms, and familiar routines in performing their jobs. Even though welfare workers may not be formally trained in social welfare, there is an ethos and culture that guides their work and the practice of their shared profession. As Sandfort found in her research,

> front-line staff develop shared knowledge and collective beliefs from their day-to-day experiences. They develop and utilize organizational resources in ways that reinforce those schemas and give rise to the unique structures of their social systems.[1]

In a fundamental way, the findings presented in chapter 4 echo the writings of Frederick Mosher in his 1968 classic, the duly celebrated *Democracy and the Public Service*.[2] Mosher argued that not only were government managers professionals, but so too were the *staff* of government organizations.[3] "They are organizationally below management," he writes, "but are often considered to be superior in educational and social terms."[4] They possess the specialized knowledge, autonomy, and professional ethos that enable them to solve problems and get the work of the agency done *correctly*. Mosher recognized that public employees in such professions as social welfare and public health possess a particular occupational orientation and develop a set of skills and knowledge that guides their work. In this sense, he described a phenomenon that contemporary researchers continue to uncover in their studies of the behaviors of government organizations at the micro level: work norms, shared knowledge, and socialization are important determinants of street-level bureaucratic behavior, as this book shows.[5]

The research presented in this book also shows that there is a tension between the goals of welfare reform and the way they are articulated by managers and supervisors in local welfare agencies. And street-level bureaucrats pick up on these tensions or conflicts. On the one hand, they recognize that welfare-to-work is a priority. Yet they also see eligibility determination as one of their key functions, placing it at the top of their list of priorities. So despite the political cries to move welfare clients off of welfare and into jobs, street-level bureaucrats recognize that they have a professional responsibility to determine effectively and efficiently an applicant's eligibility to receive cash benefits.

Maynard-Moody and Musheno make a similar, complementary point in their study of the behaviors of front-line workers. They state that

> the judgements and related actions [of front-line workers] are reached with confidence and an unblinking focus on the people who come to these workers. They deal with faces. Street-level workers do not question themselves with regard to the power they wield, nor do they seem disposed to weigh the broader implications of their actions.[6]

In this sense, front-line staff are doing their jobs the best they can, and in doing so, they inevitably fall back on their professional or work ethos, their own belief systems, their familiar work customs and routines.

We also learned that management and leadership factors may have relatively little influence on bureaucratic behavior at the front lines of service delivery. But we cannot necessarily infer from this that front-line workers are insurgent or averse to accepting management directives. On the contrary, managers and front-line staff, as even Mosher recognized, have mutually supportive roles and responsibilities that tend to converge around the clients. For instance, despite the fact that public managers face greater political pressures to tout the welfare reform goal of "welfare-to-work," their drive or motivation to ensure that

Table 5.1. Front-Line Workers' Views of Management and Leadership Practices in Local Welfare Offices, All States.

Leadership Practices	Mean	S.D.
Workers' Freedom to Raise Issues	3.8	1.3
Overall Job Satisfaction	3.2	1.2
Decision-Making Structure	2.3	1.3
Open Communication with Supervisor	4.4	1.0
Lateral Communication	4.4	0.9
Downward Communication	3.6	1.1
Supervisor Loyalty to Staff	4.0	1.3
Supervisor Creativity	3.8	1.1

$n = 196$

Scale: 1 to 5, where 1 is low and 5 is high.

welfare applicants or clients are being processed fairly and accurately for benefits is not diminished. Indeed, as we saw in chapter 3, managers continue to measure the performance of front-line workers around such eligibility determination functions as standards of promptness and error rates. We also saw, in chapter 4, that the job satisfaction of street-level bureaucrats in local welfare offices is positively correlated with management and leadership behaviors and styles (as table 5.1 also shows). Thus, management contributes to a positive and supportive work environment for street-level bureaucrats.

If street-level workers are explicitly defying neither management directives nor the rules and regulations that pervade their work, an important question remains: Are front-line workers in welfare offices at least open and amenable to the directives of their managers and supervisors? This is a critical concern and the focus of this chapter; it can provide valuable insights to organizations, specifically public managers seeking to develop measures to enhance their ability to supervise and direct their staff. Sandfort came to a similar conclusion in her research. She suggests that existing management techniques do not account for the fact that there is an informal social process based on work norms and shared knowledge that guides the work of front-line staff in welfare offices. Therefore, alternative approaches to management must be developed.[7]

Table 5.2. Response Rate of Survey Distribution, by Site (percentages).

Texas	90.91	Michigan	45.88
Masters	94.12	Wayne	19.61
Grand Prairie	92.31	Macomb	92.00
Denton	85.71	Hillsdale	66.67
Georgia	75.25	New York	80.36
SW Fulton	58.06	Albany	88.46
NW Fulton	89.47	Suffolk	73.33
Bibb	75.00		
	Total All Sites 69.93		

Public Management and Workers' Goal Perceptions about Welfare

Referring to the model presented in chapter 1, the research question addressed in this chapter is, Does management in terms of administrative capacity and behaviors in local welfare offices have an impact on the *beliefs* of front-line workers in terms of service delivery?

The dependent variables for the analysis in this section are the three goal clusters described in chapter 4: (1) "eligibility determination," (2) "employment," and (3) "diversion." However, unlike in chapter 4, these clusters are derived from the survey data, not the encounter data. As explained in chapter 1 and appendix B, 286 surveys were administered to the front-line workers at welfare offices where there is face-to-face contact with TANF applicants or clients. A total of 200 surveys were returned for a 70 percent response rate overall (see table 5.2 for breakdown by site).[8]

Front-line workers were asked to rate their perceptions or *beliefs* about the importance of eleven separate goals of welfare. A Likert-type scale ranging from 1 = "not at all" to 5 = "a great deal" was used. Based on this analysis, the three summative goal indices were constructed. Goals in the "eligibility determination" index relate to traditional goals of the welfare system: the timely and accurate processing of welfare claims. Goals in the "employment" index relate to the new welfare reform goals requiring and supporting employment. Those in the "diversion" index relate to a variety of federal and local goals to deter welfare use, prevent fraudulent claims, and discourage out-of-wedlock births.

The independent variables are primarily those included in the analysis in chapter 4: training; performance monitoring; management and leadership styles; gender, ethnicity and education of front-line workers; years working with welfare clients; and service mix.

What Affects Goal Perceptions?

Table 5.3 presents the results of the ordinary least squares (OLS) regression analyses estimating the contribution of management and leadership factors to the goal perceptions of street-level bureaucrats. As noted, goal perceptions refer to workers' responses to survey questions about how important each of the goal clusters—eligibility determination, employment, or diversion—are to them.

As the data show, several management and leadership factors emerge as important explanations for variation in staff beliefs about welfare goals. Indicators of staff training, supervision and performance monitoring, open communication styles, and participatory management were significantly and differentially associated with staff perceptions of the importance of the three clusters of goals attributes, particularly eligibility determination and diversion. This suggests that management does matter in terms of the extent to which workers acknowledge the importance of eligibility determination and diversion goals. Management mattered less for employment, except where participatory management styles were exhibited.

It is also interesting to note that the gender and ethnicity of the workers impact the degree to which they embrace the different welfare goals. The data in table 5.3 show that men are more likely to embrace the goals around welfare-to-work and diversion. The data further show that workers of color are more likely to embrace the goal of eligibility determination, while white workers are more likely to em-

Table 5.3. Management and Goal Perceptions of Street-Level Bureaucrats (OLS Multiple Regression).

Topic	Eligibility Determination	Employment	Diversion
	Beta	Beta	Beta
Supervision/Monitoring	0.23***	0.35	0.25***
Training	−0.01	0.04	0.12*
Open Communication	−0.06	−0.06	0.12*
Participatory Management	0.17**	0.21***	0.24***
Gender of Worker	−0.11	−0.17***	−0.18**
Ethnicity of Worker	−0.13*	0.14*	0.12*
Education	−0.04	−0.17***	−0.13*
Years Working with Welfare Clients	−0.01	0.06	−0.10
Service Mix	0.01	−0.03	0.01
R^2	0.10	0.19	0.24
Adjusted R^2	0.05	0.15	0.19

* $p < .10$
** $p < .05$
*** $p < .01$

brace the goals of welfare-to-work and diversion. Although beyond the scope of this research, these findings have significance for studies on representative bureaucracy or the degree to which women and people of color working at the front lines of service delivery are representing the needs and interests of women and people of color seeking welfare benefits.

How Can Public Managers Better Manage Front-Line Workers?

The findings presented in this chapter suggest that, to varying degrees, workers are open to management directives around the three goal clusters, particularly eligibility determination and diversion. But there is a dissonance when these findings are juxtaposed with those presented in chapter 4, which showed that management and leadership factors have relatively little impact on the actual *behaviors* of front-line staff. It may be recalled that the data illustrated that not management but rather such factors as professional norms and work culture impact the behaviors of workers operating at the front lines of service delivery. Scholars such as Frederick Mosher have for decades emphasized the importance of work ethic and professionalism to public administrative professions. This being the case, how are public managers able to manage their staff?

The discussion here must necessarily begin with the significance of *context*. In the private sector, for example, the answer to the aforementioned question would be relatively simple: draconian management practices are employed, whereby employees are afforded no job security or protections; intransigent, uncompliant workers are fired and, if necessary, replaced; higher salaries are paid to new staff to motivate them to perform the desired tasks in order to reach the expected outcomes. In the context of welfare, the stated goal would be finding jobs for welfare clients (or getting people off welfare) and the performance measures for front-line staff would revolve around job placement (or caseload reductions) with concomitant rewards or punishments depending upon whether or not the targeted goal is met.

Parenthetically, very few states or localities contract their TANF services to private, for-profit firms. And even in those instances where certain case management functions such as eligibility determination have been contracted out to such firms, the actual disbursement of the cash assistance must be made by a public agency. For example, in Palm Beach County, Florida, the for-profit contractor, Affiliated Computer Services, Inc., is responsible for all case management and processing functions, including TANF eligibility determination; but the Florida Department of Children and Families makes the benefit payments.[9] Nevertheless, the disbursement of funds is based on how employees at the private sector firm process welfare applicants or clients for benefits. The private sector firm, then, has de facto control over the cash assistance program. It should further be noted that by law, only public or government employees can determine eligibility for food stamps and Medicaid.

In the public sector, of course, the task of managing is not that simple. The context of government employment, with its various legal, political, and unparalleled organizational constraints, makes the task of managing staff, particularly those guided by work norms and professional principles, much more complicated. Thus, for all the important reasons, the private sector or business management gurus cannot guide us here. The same goes for those espousing the "New Public Management" principles and philosophy—with its endorsement of corporate practices, it follows closely on the heels of business administration.

By first recognizing the value of context, the task then becomes one of effectively managing change in *occupational* culture at the street level of bureaucracy. Traditionally, culture, in particular organization culture, has taken on a host of meanings.[10] Schein, one of the leading scholars on organization culture, has defined the concept as a

> pattern of shared basic assumptions that [a] group learned as it solved its problems of external adaptation and internal integration, that has worked well enough to be considered valid and, therefore, to be taught to new members as the correct way to perceive, think, and feel in relation to those problems.[11]

Most of these definitions emanate from corporate sector practices and business administration scholars and pundits (for example, Osborne and Gaebler).[12] Yet, some students of public management, as Khademian has observed, have "accepted and adopted this 'corporate culture' approach to organizational culture." As she appropriately warns for public management, however,

> the value of organizational culture for management practitioners and scholars might rest not with its potential as a management tool per se, but as a means to understand the context (constraints and opportunities) within which managers manage and *how* management matters.[13]

Broadly stated, for management to matter at the street level of bureaucracy, public managers must recognize and understand *not only* the constraints and opportunities posed by the organizational culture (i.e., the norms and ideologies characterizing the organization *where* workers do their jobs), but also the constraints and opportunities posed by the *occupational* culture—the ideologies and norms that characterize what workers do and how they do it.[14] Only then, argues Khademian, can culture and work norms become a controllable, "*manageable* variable for bringing about organizational reform."[15]

At the broad organizational level, the key constraint has perhaps been best identified by Kane and Bane, who argued that reforming the welfare system

> is not simply a matter of changing eligibility rules. Rather, it represents a dramatic shift from an organizational culture in which the dominant ethos is centered around *eligibility and compliance* to one in which clients and welfare workers are engaged in the common tasks of finding work, arranging for child care, and so on.[16]

As noted previously, at some level it was recognized that a bureaucratic system that had been operating with an eligibility-compliance culture for over sixty years could not readily be changed.[17] And so the principal component of welfare reform—welfare to work—was shifted to separate agencies or units to ensure effective delivery of employment services.

But, as seen from the findings presented in this book, perhaps the more critical undertaking is to recognize the constraints presented by the culture not of bureaucracy but of *street-level* bureaucracy. The values of professional norms, work routines, and customs are so inculcated in street-level workers that they may not even be consciously aware of their presence. An analogy might be seen in the significance and value of our nationality and cultural upbringing: these factors imbue and help define who we are, but we don't really stop to think about the fundamental ways in which they influence our daily personal lives and work behaviors.

Despite the constraints posed by the culture of street-level bureaucracy, the task of managing street-level bureaucrats is not an impossible one. Nor is redirecting their behaviors. We have already learned that open, participatory styles of management induce positive responses from street-level workers. So, too, does a high quality of supervision and performance monitoring. These management features are perhaps the foremost requisites.

It is also necessary for managers to understand clearly that it is perfectly logical for street-level workers to adhere to their work customs and professional norms. These factors undoubtedly make their jobs more "manageable" in the sense that such factors are characterized by stability, certainty, and uniformity.

Investigating opportunities for change, however, is not to be overlooked. One need only look at the vast body of literature in other disciplines where management has sought to change the behaviors of professionals within organizations. The medical sciences and engineering, for instance, provide useful examples of how professionals have been managed and directed into desired behaviors.[18]

Perhaps one of the most challenging groups of professionals to manage—aside from, let's say, tenured professors—is physicians. Highly trained and specialized, these professionals are accustomed to a great deal of autonomy, making decisions about the health and overall well-being of their clients based on their medical expertise. They are self-directed and their values, ethical codes, and professional norms ensure that they will pursue the best health interests of their clients, sometimes without much thought to the cost of the care. Is it remotely possible to change the behaviors or practices of physicians? As many have reported in such prestigious medical journals as the *Journal of the American Medical Association* and *The New England Journal of Medicine*, the answer is that while it is difficult, it is possible.

There are a number of areas where hospital administrators have found it necessary to attempt to change physician practices. For example, administrators and managers may seek to ensure that their physicians are ordering certain laboratory tests (e.g., diagnostic tests), are relying on new treatment programs, or are working to reduce unnecessary testing (e.g., chest radiographic tests). The reasons for such actions, from the standpoint of the manager or administrator, may be to contain costs or, a related matter, to eliminate duplicative or outdated services and treatments. Over the span of several decades, practicing and teaching physicians have offered several types of what they call "interventions" to help change physicians' behaviors. While front-line workers in welfare agencies are professionals of a different kind, the tools and processes for changing the behaviors of physicians and engineers can provide some insight into how welfare administrators and managers can redirect street-level bureaucratic behavior.

Education

A number of studies point to the importance of educating professionals about "cause and effect"—that is to say, addressing specific types of behaviors (e.g., lack of willingness to order diagnostic tests) and the outcomes they are associated with (e.g., injudicious, costly treatments).[19]

As noted, professionals often engage in behaviors and practices that are familiar to them and represent the standard way of doing things. By setting up workshops with managers and staff to discuss the consequences of various behaviors, professional staff are able to see the broader picture of the actual services delivered by their organizations; this process also leads to consensus building.[20] Moreover, strategies for producing desired results can be identified and explored. As Lynn has pointed out, it is critical to encourage explicit self-consciousness of goal conflicts among staff to "make it more likely that you can manage it."[21] Even though resources may be scarce and the process may be time-consuming, the regular convening of these types of meetings or workshops can assist managers and administrators in their efforts to redirect the behaviors of their staff.

Related *formal* training may also be an important strategy for influencing work behaviors. Earlier in this chapter, it was reported that training can affect the views of front-line workers about welfare goals. In chapter 3, it was reported that formal as opposed to informal training may be a more effective strategy for changing worker behaviors in that it ensures that there is some uniformity and standardization in the content of the training provided to all staff members. Informal training like on-the-job training reinforces learned work norms and customs, thereby fostering, as Schein argues, the "old, familiar ways."[22] Although cost constraints often preclude formal training programs, a genuine desire to influence street-level bureaucratic behavior may be worth the investment in the long run.

Participation by the Professionals

Many have made the point that efforts to change the behaviors of professionals such as physicians cannot be imposed by outsiders; they must involve the professionals themselves.[23] As Greco and Eisenberg have argued in their study of changing physicians' practices, outside consultants may not share physicians' professional or personal concerns. Moreover:

> Theories of change and common sense suggest that physicians will oppose changes they perceive as threatening to their livelihood, self-esteem, sense of competence, or autonomy. Thus, interventions that decrease physicians' decision-making authority, reduce their income, challenge their professional judgments, or appear to compromise patient care are more likely to fail. According to these notions, involving physicians in the effort to effect change should make change less threatening.[24]

In short, efforts to change the behaviors and practices of professionals must necessarily afford the professionals a role in the process. And the group must reach agreement about what the goals are. Quality-improvement efforts, including the now somewhat defunct Total Quality Management (TQM) programs, which demand participation from the workers, are one viable strategy here; for one thing, the focus is on improving the quality of services to the clients as opposed to controlling costs. Furthermore, the emphasis is on outcome, not process. That is to say, there is no preconceived notion that practices must change in some specific way in order to improve service delivery.[25]

Continuous Feedback

Consistent monitoring of whether and how the goals are being achieved is essential. Feedback entails providing professional staff with information about how their practices affect services and client outcome. It also provides information to both management and staff as to what changes may still be necessary to reach the agreed upon goals.

A safe, supportive climate must be set so that workers and managers alike remain continually open to communication, praise—and criticism too. Time must be provided to those receiving the feedback, so that they can respond accordingly.[26] As Solomon and his colleagues found, continuous monitoring has been recognized as an effective strategy for quality improvement and behavior change in health care settings.[27]

Administrative Interventions

Some have argued that should all else fail, administrative interventions may still work. Greco and Eisenberg point out that

> At one extreme, changes in behavior can simply be encouraged either by creating barriers to undesired practices (for example, requiring the approval of a specialist for certain tests or medications) or by reducing barriers to desired practices (for example, by simplifying order forms).[28]

For social workers, this could mean greater micro-management by welfare managers and administrators. Of course, this would require considerable investment of resources, especially time. And while administrators and managers face legal barriers to completely overhauling the application or recertification process in welfare offices, what with its myriad forms and cumbersome interview processes, they may be able to simplify paperwork for eligibility determination, say, while increasing the paperwork or face-to-face time needed for employment counseling or coaching. Again, this will almost certainly require the valuable resource of time (as well as a heavy dose of creativity), but the point is that change is possible if there is a commitment by management and by those who control the purse strings. Obviously, if the desire is to keep people off of welfare, no changes to the eligibility process are necessary, since the onerous process of interviewing and filling out forms already serves the purpose of deterring people from coming onto welfare. Perhaps this was, after all, the goal of welfare reform.

In sum, context is extremely important for public management, especially around efforts to direct the activities and practices of street-level bureaucrats. It may be the sine qua non for management to matter at the street level of bureaucracy. While it may be the case that management factors are *outweighed* by such factors as work norms and professionalism, public managers are nonetheless capable of redirecting the behaviors of their front-line workers. The efficacy of public managers in directing front-line staff may hinge on their commitment to developing appropriate "interventions" (e.g., running continuous workshops). The cost of such activities, measured mostly in time, may be high, but the ultimate benefits derived justify the use of this valuable resource.

CHAPTER SIX

What Are Welfare Workers Doing at the Front Lines?

The role of public management, as seen in this book, may not be as salient at the street level of bureaucracy as it is at other levels. Another way to look at this is that certain aspects of the jobs of front-line workers are not as easily supervised, precisely because of the discretion possessed by the workers. Given these circumstances, what exactly are the street-level bureaucrats doing in welfare agencies, in this era of postreform? While previously we learned that eligibility determination comprises a large part of the street-level worker's job, this chapter illustrates in greater detail the various activities of front-line workers in local welfare offices. It relies on the encounter data—in the form of transcripts—which capture the interactions between street-level workers and TANF applicants and clients.

The Activities of Welfare Workers and Clients

Data were presented in chapter 4 on the frequency with which the three goal clusters were discussed by street-level workers in their interviews or encounters with welfare applicants or clients. These data showed that eligibility determination was a topic of discussion in 50.1 percent of the encounters; employment was a topic of discussion in 33.1 percent of the encounters, diversion in 15.9 percent. Table 6.1 presents these data by state; the data confirm that eligibility determination issues are addressed most frequently across states.

Table 6.1. Frequency with Which Topics Are Discussed in Welfare Departments, by State.

	Georgia			New York		
	Topic of Discussion			Topic of Discussion		
Topic	(%)	Mean	S.D.	(%)	Mean	S.D.
Eligibility Determination	43.0	4.50	4.1	58.0	4.50	4.10
Employment	37.0	3.90	3.27	25.0	1.98	4.05
Diversion	20.0	2.08	2.88	17.0	1.28	1.97
	$n = 193$ encounters			$n = 301$ encounters		

	Michigan			Texas		
	Topic of Discussion			Topic of Discussion		
Topic	(%)	Mean	S.D.	(%)	Mean	S.D.
Eligibility Determination	54.0	11.29	8.59	47.0	9.73	9.61
Employment	35.0	7.48	6.82	34.0	7.19	7.05
Diversion	11.0	2.36	3.16	19.0	3.91	3.91
	$n = 147$ encounters			$n = 89$ encounters		

What Topics Are Being Addressed?

A more comprehensive breakdown of the topics discussed by welfare workers at the front-line level is presented in table 6.2. It shows the frequency with which individual topics were mentioned at least once by welfare workers in their interactions with TANF applicants or clients. One interesting observation is the relatively low frequency with which certain key issues under welfare reform are discussed. For example, time limits across states are a topic of discussion in only 9.6 percent of the encounters. A comparison by state indicates that street-level welfare workers in Texas discuss time limits more than the other states (37.1 percent).

The fact that welfare recipients now face time limits on cash assistance is an important piece of information to convey to TANF recipients. But it appears that time limits are not discussed very frequently in the interview for TANF benefits.[1] When it is discussed, it is done in

Table 6.2. Frequency of Topics Discussed in Encounters, by State (percentages).

Topic	Georgia	Michigan	New York	Texas	Total Encounters
Child Care (e.g., Will you need it when you find a job?)	66.3	55.1	27.2	53.9	46.4
Child Support	40.9	31.3	22.6	40.4	31.4
Earned Income	1.0	2.0	1.3	5.6	1.9
Earnings Disregards	0.5	3.4	0.7	0.0	1.1
Emergency Assistance	0.0	11.6	4.3	1.1	4.2
Entitlement	4.7	17.7	2.3	19.1	8.1
Family Cap	11.4	0.0	0.0	0.0	3.0
Family Planning	7.8	0.0	0.3	2.2	2.5
Family Problems	20.7	19.7	14.3	22.5	18.1
Fraud	3.1	1.4	6.0	4.5	4.1
Health, Disability, and Mental Health	16.1	42.9	18.3	15.7	22.3
One-Time Diversion Assistance	0.0	6.1	1.3	1.1	1.9
Parenting	1.6	4.8	0.7	10.1	2.9
Personal Responsibility Agreement	17.6	12.2	0.3	29.2	10.8
Pregnancy	12.4	13.6	11.6	13.5	12.5
Sanctions (Discussing/ Threatening)	10.4	14.3	19.9	14.6	15.6
Substance Abuse	7.3	6.8	6.3	7.9	6.8
Time Limits	11.4	6.8	1.7	37.1	9.6
Transportation (e.g., Does client own a car?)	51.3	57.8	19.6	61.8	40.8

such a perfunctory manner that the client may not understand the implications. The following excerpt from an encounter in a Dallas, Texas, office of the Department of Human Services is illustrative:

WORKER: . . . and, um, you're registered to vote?

APPLICANT: Uh huh.

WORKER: Go ahead and sign this for me so they will know that I asked you about voting. Sign right there, OK? You have to sign and date it. I need to give you a card to sign. This is a . . . a personal responsibility app that says that this TANF is temporary. You need to sign and sign and date that there. Cause you, you know you will be on time limit.

APPLICANT: Uh huh.

WORKER: I don't know what your time limit will be but once you get your time limits, then you will no longer be getting TANF. I need for you to sign right there. Was this little boy [*referring to applicant's son, who is present*] also in Mahia High School?

APPLICANT: De Mayer?

The topic of time limits here was glossed over, and it seems evident that the significance of the time limit didn't quite sink in with the applicant.

Table 6.2 also shows that the Personal Responsibility Agreement (PRA) is a topic of discussion in only 10.8 percent of the total encounters. As explained more fully in chapters 2 and 3, the PRA is the written agreement between the client and the government (or TANF program) that clients are required to sign and date as a condition of eligibility for benefits. The agreement states that the client agrees that: (1) TANF assistance is temporary; (2) TANF is a work program; (3) it is the client's responsibility to get and keep work, and (4) the client accepts responsibility for themselves and their children. In Texas, the PRA is a topic of discussion in 29.2 percent of the encounters, whereas in New York, it is a topic in only 0.3 percent. Overall, the PRA is also discussed perfunctorily, but even when the worker seeks to stress the importance of the PRA, clients don't appear to understand or register its significance, as seen in the following encounter from a Family Independence Agency (FIA) office in Macomb, Michigan:

WORKER: Okay. I'm going to mark down here all the assets and it's also pertaining to your parents. . . . You're going to have to sign this form. It has to do with the personal contract. We have to have this at application and at review. Okay, while you're sitting there, you have to read this section and you should really read the entire form. But this is what really pertains to you right here and then you have to initial it here, that's stating that you understand it and then if you have any questions, don't do it until you ask me those questions. I want you to understand what your responsibilities are when you come in here applying for cash assistance, okay? And then you have to sign down there, okay?

[*Pause*]

APPLICANT: [*Talks to her baby*]

WORKER: [*Worker uses computer—long pause*]

APPLICANT: [*Preoccupied with crying baby*]

WORKER: Did you understand what this was saying?

APPLICANT: Yeah. [*Continues to talk to baby*]

WORKER: Okay, that's your copy there. Okay, I'm going to get all the documents and I'm going to go Xerox this and then I'm going to schedule you for the Work First meeting, okay? I should be right back.

The applicant, preoccupied with her baby, signed the PRA without having read or understood its content.

Interestingly, workers are required to ask if the applicant is pregnant, yet the data show that workers do not inquire about pregnancy 100 percent of the time (see table 6.2).[2] When the worker does ask about pregnancy, the worker will generally offer some comments, which may be construed as judgment, rebuke, or counsel. Consider the following encounter from the Department of Social Services in Suffolk County, New York:

WORKER: You're not [*pause*] pregnant?

APPLICANT: No. Bite your tongue!

WORKER: I know. [*both laugh*]

APPLICANT: I like how you said, "You're not . . . pregnant?" [*laughs*]

WORKER: Usually I go through this whole thing, and the client says "Oh, by the way, I'm going to have another baby."

APPLICANT: [*inaudible*]

WORKER: . . . I see this every day. It's very difficult. Every once in a while I get hooked and [really upset about what's happening to my clients]. It's hard.

APPLICANT: That's what happened to me. [*explains story of how she lost her job and is having difficulty with child care*]

WORKER: Yeah, it's hectic. Very difficult. My daughter has difficulty with child care, and she doesn't know what to do. She has two very difficult boys. They were thrown out of day care.

APPLICANT: Oh boy! [*laughs*] Didn't even make it to school and got kicked out.

WORKER: A play group!

APPLICANT: My boy's never been in day care. But he's hot-headed.

The encounter shows the tension around the "pregnancy" question, and, because the applicant is not pregnant, a friendly badinage ensues.

Entitlement is also a critical topic under welfare reform, because the TANF program ended the entitlement status for cash assistance. As with time limits, this is important information for the client. Yet, entitlement is discussed overall in only 8.1 percent of the encounters. Texas and Michigan address it more often than the other states. It is unclear if clients even understand the subtle nuances of "entitlement" as opposed to simply receiving cash benefits; in most cases, the worker may not fully explain its actual meaning. The following encounter from the Division of Family and Children Services (DFCS) in Bibb County, Georgia, makes this clear:

WORKER: When you apply for TANF, TANF is no longer an entitlement even if you have children under 19.

APPLICANT: What you mean, for TANF money?

WORKER: They have a four-year limit. You could only receive it for four years, no more.

APPLICANT: He's [her son is] 16 now.

WORKER: You and your children live at [address]?

APPLICANT: Right.

WORKER: And the telephone number is [phone number]?

APPLICANT: Yes.

WORKER: Do you want to go ahead and apply?

APPLICANT: Yes.

Interestingly, as discussed in greater detail in chapter 2, New York State has a constitutional provision that guarantees cash assistance to those qualifying for aid, even if the five-year TANF time limit has been exhausted. The "Safety Net" program mandates, under the state's constitution, state-local general assistance to "aid, care, and support the needy" and for "the protection and promotion of the health of the inhabitants of the state." Yet in only two of the encounters in New York was the Safety Net program discussed as an option. In one case, the client raised it. In the other one, the worker did, as seen in the following encounter from the Department of Social Services office in Albany, New York (the applicant in this case is male):

WORKER: What's going on?

APPLICANT: I was working but I got fired.

WORKER: What happened?

APPLICANT: My boss wanted me to do a supervisor's job, but they wouldn't pay me more. I said no, and they fired me.

WORKER: Where is your son?

APPLICANT: He's in Job Corps. He comes home on weekends.

WORKER: You are probably going to be denied. You're going to have to apply for Safety Net because your son is not living with you. You are sanctionable because you got fired.

APPLICANT: I'll be right back, I need my glasses. [*Applicant goes to the waiting area to discuss the application with his girlfriend; returns in five minutes.*]

WORKER: Sign here.

APPLICANT: OK.

WORKER: I'll be right back. [*Worker leaves to write a denial notice; worker returns in fifteen minutes.*]

WORKER: I talked to your employer [*worker actually* did not *telephone the former employer*]. We can't help you. You are eligible for Medicaid. You are sanctioned for 90 days for cash and 60 days for food stamps. It would be easier if you found a job. Other cleaning agencies are hiring.

APPLICANT: I want to talk to someone else.

WORKER: You left your job. You are sanctioned.

[*Applicant reiterates the problem he had at his job*]

WORKER: You need to get these documents in for Medicaid.

APPLICANT: If I get no money, I'm screwed. Can I see your supervisor?

WORKER: Sure.

[*Twenty minutes pass. Worker gets another worker who poses as a supervisor.*]

WORKER 2: Hi. What's up?

APPLICANT: I'm not getting money. I worked at a job. They wanted me
to be a supervisor, but they didn't pay me more, so I said no and was
fired.

WORKER 2: Now you have no job. You can't refuse available work and
come here asking for assistance.

APPLICANT: What can I do?

WORKER 2: Find a job. The sanction is ninety days from the last day
you worked. You last worked on 7/24. You can reapply on September 8th.

APPLICANT: Can I do Medicaid?

WORKER 2: Yes. I'll send the worker back.

WORKER: I've got to keep a copy of this for your application. You're
all set. Bring in the documents listed here. [*Hands client a list of necessary documentation*]

APPLICANT: OK.

In this case, the Safety Net program was mentioned, but the worker
was dishonest about calling the applicant's former employer and also
in presenting a coworker to the applicant in the guise of a supervisor.
The encounter also illustrates the manner in which a worker can rely
on discretionary powers to deny aid to an applicant.

It is also interesting to note, as seen in table 6.2, that one-time
payments are not discussed very often. One-time payments are intended to divert applicants from coming on to TANF for long periods
of time. As the data show, one-time diversion assistance was a topic of
discussion in only 1.9 percent of the encounters, indicating that
overall, workers did not seek to divert TANF applicants with this
tactic.

Finally, the earnings disregard, which allows a certain amount of income from employment to be disregarded in terms of benefit calculation, is also important under welfare reform. It provides an assurance or guarantee of sorts to welfare applicants or clients that they can continue to receive welfare benefits even if they are working. Yet of all the topics discussed in these four states, it is addressed the least frequently, in only 1.1 percent of the encounters. In Michigan, which has a relatively generous earnings disregard, welfare workers addressed it in only 3.4 percent of the encounters.

What Activities Are Occurring?

Table 6.3 presents a breakdown of the frequency with which street-level workers in welfare offices engaged in various activities. The data show that eligibility determination activities are the most common. In 80.8 percent of the encounters, workers collect information on the circumstances of TANF applicants or clients; in 63.6 percent, they explain rules and requirements; in 53.7 percent, the workers advise or provide information on benefits programs; in 51.2 percent, workers verify the information provided by clients; and in 45.9 percent of the encounters, welfare staff work with clients to complete and sign forms. By comparison, in only 12.5 percent of the encounters do welfare workers provide TANF clients or applicants with job services, and in only 9.6 percent of the encounters do they assess employment.

Topics Discussed in Conjunction with TANF

It is also interesting to compare the frequency of topics discussed by welfare workers when the TANF program is specifically addressed with applicants or clients. Table 6.4 presents these cross-tabulations. When TANF is specifically addressed, the topics discussed most frequently across all states are child care and transportation. It is also noteworthy that certain topics are addressed much more frequently in Texas than in the other states, including transportation, child care, the PRA, and time limits. The topic addressed least frequently, when TANF is dis-

Table 6.3. Frequency of Worker Activities, by State (percentages).

Topic	Georgia	Michigan	New York	Texas	Total
Acting on Sanctions	21.8	30.6	13.0	34.8	21.5
Advising/Informing about Benefits Programs	51.8	75.5	40.2	67.4	53.7
Assessing Employment	19.2	12.2	3.2	4.5	9.6
Collecting Info. on Circumstances	74.6	87.8	81.4	80.9	80.8
Collecting Documents	16.1	19.7	10.0	16.9	14.4
Completing, Signing Forms	56.5	61.2	23.9	71.9	45.9
Exempting from Work	8.8	6.8	5.0	14.6	7.5
Explaining Rules, Requirements	67.9	81.0	48.8	75.3	63.6
Providing Job Service	9.8	25.9	4.7	22.5	12.5
Verifying Info. Provided by Client	49.2	56.5	46.8	61.8	51.2

See appendix E for fuller description of Activity Codes.

cussed, is one-time diversion assistance (in 0.4 percent of the encounters) followed by earnings disregards (in 0.5 percent of the encounters), family cap (in 0.8 percent of the encounters) and family planning (in 1.0 percent of the encounters). Interestingly, it would appear that frontline workers do not seek to divert applicants from coming on to TANF with one-time diversion payments.

In addition, welfare workers provide job services to applicants or clients in only 1.6 percent of the encounters when TANF is the topic being addressed, as indicated in table 6.4. Corresponding with results presented earlier, the important "employment" function of providing job services under TANF is not addressed very frequently by welfare workers. These services are no doubt provided more frequently by front-line staff in the work or employment agencies.

Referrals to Mandatory Activities

Table 6.5 provides data on the frequency with which street-level workers send TANF clients or applicants to certain mandatory activities as a condition of qualifying for welfare benefits. The most striking

Table 6.4. Frequency of Topics Addressed with TANF, by State (percentages).

Topic	Georgia	Michigan	New York	Texas	Total
Child Care	18.1	13.6	4.0	36.0	13.6
Earnings Disregards	0.0	2.0	0.3	0.0	0.5
Entitlement	2.6	5.4	0.3	16.9	4.0
Work Exemptions	1.0	0.0	1.3	10.1	2.1
Family Cap	3.1	0.0	0.0	0.0	0.8
Family Planning	2.6	0.0	0.0	2.2	1.0
One-Time Diversion Assistance	0.0	2.0	0.0	0.0	0.4
Providing Job Service	0.0	2.7	0.3	7.9	1.6
PRA	5.7	4.8	0.0	23.6	5.3
Time Limits	4.1	4.1	0.3	22.5	4.8
Transportation	13.5	14.3	2.7	37.1	12.1

observation is the low frequency with which applicants or clients are referred to mandatory activities. Certainly, if workers accepted the goal of diversion, or keeping people from coming on to welfare, they could require applicants to undergo drug rehabilitation or attend counseling sessions on, say, family problems more often. Instead, the workers rarely send clients to mandatory activities, as indicated in table 6.5.

What Are the Clients Requesting?

In addition to the activities of street-level bureaucrats, the encounter data also captured certain actions or requests made by the clients. Table 6.6 presents these data. Not surprisingly, the requests or actions of

Table 6.5. Frequency with Which Worker Sends Clients to Mandatory Activity, by State (percentages).

Reason for Mandatory Activity	Georgia	Michigan	New York	Texas	Total
Family Planning	1.0	0.0	0.0	0.0	0.3
Family Problems	0.0	0.0	1.0	0.0	0.4
Health, Disability, Mental Health	2.1	1.4	0.3	1.1	1.1
Immunization of Children	0.5	0.0	0.3	3.4	0.7
Parenting	0.0	0.0	0.0	2.2	0.3
Substance Abuse	2.1	0.7	1.7	0.0	1.4

Table 6.6. Frequency of Client or Applicant Requests or Actions, by State (percentages).

Client Requests/Actions	Georgia	Michigan	New York	Texas	Total
Declining Benefits	1.6	2.7	1.7	2.2	1.9
Disclosing Problems	31.6	52.4	30.9	48.3	37.5
Inquiring about Rights	0.5	0.0	0.7	2.2	0.7
Inquiring about Rules or Benefits	33.2	48.3	33.6	59.6	39.6
Requesting Other Assistance or Service	3.1	5.4	3.7	3.4	3.8
Underground Economy	0.5	1.4	0.3	1.1	0.7

See appendix E for fuller description of Activity Codes.

clients occurring most frequently are inquiring about rules and benefits (in 39.6 percent of the encounters) and disclosing problems (in 37.5 percent of the encounters).[3] The following encounter in the Division of Family and Children Services (DFCS), Northwest Fulton County, Georgia, illustrates what can occur when a client discloses a problem:

APPLICANT: Would it be possible to get anything today?

WORKER: No. It takes about one week. How did you get this card if you never got food stamps recently?

APPLICANT: That's not a food stamp card.

WORKER: Oh. This is your social security benefits card. It looks just like the EBT [Electronic Benefits Transfer]. Okay, it can go downstairs. Do you have any relatives in town?

APPLICANT: Yes. [name], she lives in Decatur.

WORKER: You have to stay in Fulton [County] to get food stamps.

APPLICANT: No. You asked if I had any relatives. I'm living in a shelter.

WORKER: Do you have a checking or savings?

APPLICANT: No.

WORKER: Do you have a vehicle?

APPLICANT: I don't have nothing. TV, radio. . . .

This client is clearly in need of immediate help. However, as is often the case, the worker does not, or cannot, due to organizational or programmatic constraints, respond to the applicant's needs or interests.

Do Clients Ever Decline Benefits?

Table 6.6 also shows that in only a small number of instances did applicants or clients decline benefits. In general, this happens when an applicant declines TANF assistance, for example, but pursues benefits such as food stamps and/or Medicaid. For example, in Hillsdale, Michigan, an applicant declined food stamps as well as cash benefits because, with income from her job, the benefit would be relatively small:

WORKER: You don't want cash assistance?

APPLICANT: Well, I'm only getting $52 or something.

WORKER: That's, that's good, you know I think it's wise if you can get by without it.

APPLICANT: Yeah.

WORKER: Hey, it's wise. Because Michigan is not observing the five-year lifetime limit right now but in the future . . . and it's like preserving your eligibility for the future if you need them later.

APPLICANT: Plus, it's only $52, so I thought. The main thing I need is the medical because I don't have medical right now and being a diabetic, that's [inaudible].

WORKER: Yep. Okay, you got him down here as eating with you but not requesting benefits.

APPLICANT: Right.

WORKER: It's either one or the other for food stamps. If he's eating with you he has to be. . . .

APPLICANT: I don't even get that any more, though.

WORKER: The food stamps?

APPLICANT: No.

WORKER: You said you still want food stamps?

APPLICANT: Yeah. But. We don't get it. The cash out is gone since his income, you know?

WORKER: Okay. All right. Okay.

APPLICANT: So. Really it's only medical.

WORKER: But you're requesting it. So you don't really want it?

APPLICANT: No, not really.

WORKER: Whoops. We'll cross off and let you initial. I was thinking you
were still getting and you were requesting it, so.

APPLICANT: No.

In another instance, an applicant for assistance in Denton, Texas, refused day care because she didn't trust the quality of care provided. The
following is an excerpt from that encounter, indicating why assistance
was not sought by the applicant:

WORKER: Maybe get a car, would that be an advantage of working?
I mean, once you got, you know, got where you could get a car.
I mean, even if it's a used car; that's somethin' that's gonna get
you from Point A to Point B. Get the kids to day care, get to
work.

APPLICANT: No day care.

WORKER: No day care?

APPLICANT: My kids [*won't be in? inaudible*] in day care.

WORKER: So what are you going to do?

APPLICANT: I have a mother-in-law, basically, or what would have been
my mother-in-law, my mother and my grandmother who all have
their own schedules. My mother doesn't work; she's got a seven-
year-old and a five-year-old that she takes care of, and my kids are
four and two.

WORKER: OK.

APPLICANT: And they, I refuse for them to go to day care.

WORKER: Well, you're very lucky that you have family that you can take
the kids to.

APPLICANT: Yeah. If I didn't, I'd, you know, might be a little bit different but I still, I hate day care.

WORKER: OK. And not all are bad, they really aren't. I mean, I know. . . .

APPLICANT: And I know quite a few of them and I know that, you
know, a lot of behind-the-scenes things do happen and a lot of what
they don't tell the parents and, you know, plus also, you know, with
my grandmother and my mother and somebody who I can trust to
watch my children. If my kid gets sick, they know how to reach me

but I don't have to get up and run and lose my job and I've known plenty of mothers who have lost their job because oh, this kid has a fever, you have to come pick her up. And fever's what, 99.4, that's not a fever. A fever's 100.1. Anything above that, a child should go to the hospital. If it's not the, you know, it's just, you know, some kids run temperature and my son always runs 99.4 all the time, all the time. His temperature is never normal. So I'm just like, uh, I'm glad he's not in day care.

Working "Under the Table"

It is also not surprising that there are so few instances of "underground economy" being disclosed. This is where the applicant or client discloses work or income that is not reported for income tax purposes. The following two encounters, each from a different state, illustrate the unique ways in which street-level bureaucrats handle a client's disclosure of undeclared income.

Encounter 1: Division of Family and Children Services (DFCS), Northwest Fulton County:

WORKER: Okay, it shows here that we have to verify past employment, especially if it's been within the past year. Are you still with Krystal Company?

APPLICANT: My last job was with Enterprise.

WORKER: When did that end?

APPLICANT: January.

WORKER: Do you have your separation letter?

APPLICANT: Yes. I have it at home.

WORKER: Okay, so you just get paid cash when you do hair?

APPLICANT: Yes, but it's not a steady thing.

WORKER: How much do you estimate you make a week?

APPLICANT: About $100.

WORKER: If you continue braiding, I'll need you to start keeping track. . . .

APPLICANT: It's always spent before I get it.

WORKER: I know how that goes.

APPLICANT: On Pampers, wipes, household items, bus fare to look for a job. It's really hard to look for a job without a GED and no job training.

The worker in this case appears relatively lenient about the money—which is a small amount—that the applicant earns from hair braiding. The worker even shows some understanding about how the cash is spent so quickly on essential items such as baby diapers.

Encounter 2: Family Independence Agency (FIA), Detroit, Michigan:

WORKER: How much money did you make this past week with the holiday doing hair?

APPLICANT: I would say like $30. Cause I only did like three heads, ten-dollar heads, three little girls. A lot of little kids' hair I do for free, especially those that I've known for years. It's a lot of times a gift for them.

WORKER: Now you just told me not too long ago when the holiday comes up and it was Easter and you know Easter is a big holiday, let's be honest now.

APPLICANT: I know, I know that's what I am doing. I really only made about $30. Like I said if they had to have a hairdo I basically did it for free, seriously.

WORKER: You just sat at home and said, Oh I'm going to do your hair for free?

APPLICANT: No, no, because it's basically like a family thing. I was cooking with their moms too and basically we were spending the holiday together. You know we were cooking, we did a little shopping as a family.

WORKER: I'm going to tell you you're going to have to report that income and it's going to have to be budgeted. You also had the issue of the license. What are you going to do about that? You could have been got your license, let's be realistic.

APPLICANT: I know that I have had setbacks.

WORKER: I'm not talking about the setbacks; I'm talking about when you were referred to Work First you could have went into the program, they could have assisted you with taking the test and getting prepared to get that license. The state would have did that. They also would have helped you open up your own business through Detroit Institute and I looked in your case, you've been referred a lot. So. . . .

APPLICANT: I was being lazy.

WORKER: It wasn't a real setback when the state is offering to pay some of those expenses. Now c'mon, you been over to JVS [Jewish Vocational Services] with Miss Barbie.

APPLICANT: I didn't speak on the cosmetology issue, I didn't know that.

WORKER: When we come in there and do the orientation, they always talk about that, they always do, along with the supportive services. And I'm telling you, looking in your case and everything, you're going to have to be realistic. This is not a game and even though you may be doing hair on the side and everything at any given time, someone could, you could be kicked out, the landlord could put you out because you're using that as a place of business. Or someone could get upset if you did something wrong to their hair but realistically you're going to have to think about the long-term effects of being on welfare and what it is doing to your children as well as to you. If you would had went ahead and followed through with the requirements set up by Work First just like how we are sitting here now, I wouldn't even be sitting here with you, you would have your own business like some of the other customers who came through here who did hair. You've got to put forth an effort. And it's not a thing about like, a lot of times people say I couldn't get a break, it's this, it's that, no one was willing to help me, but the state has been willing to help. They have been willing to help and life is too short. And the way the city of Detroit is moving and the way the other areas are moving, in the state of Michigan everything is on a upswing. People are being pushed out of neighborhoods into certain other neighborhoods, so housing is very expensive and you gotta pull it together. I mean, it's not easy for those of us who come in here to work. We've got people in here who have children, four or five children who used to be just like you sitting on the other side, but you have to have something within you to push you. You can say all day that you love your children and everything, everybody loves their children but besides love you gotta give them something else and you gotta do something. You got two girls here, five and three. Life isn't going to stop, and you want them to be successful. And right now they're at the age where if you went back to school and had to do some types of studying and get your GED to get your license, you could do it because you don't have five children, you don't have eight children, okay? You don't have little babies. But you gotta push yourself. We've got a young lady in here that we're going to submit her to be profiled in a magazine, all on FIA. Because she's a mother with eight children, lives over here on the east side you know, northeast side, gets up every morning, works at Metro Airport at six o'clock, starting at six o'clock with eight children and has not missed a beat and has been doing this for quite some time. Not six months, she has been doing this for almost a year and a half. That's a success story. Okay, working at Burger King and even though some people look down at fast food and everything but you gotta start somewhere. You got a good start. You went to school for cosmetology. You been doing hair on the side. All you need is your GED and to go through with some of the courses that are available through the state. And really this is the last straw, because when you get to me, that's it. This is it. When you get to certain workers up here in the office that's it, this is it, they're phasing it out. We're project zero. So I'm going to ask you what steps are you going to take. Because it's just going to be just like general assistance. People thought they weren't going to cut out the general assistance program, they thought they weren't going to cut out mental health, but they did. So I want to know from you what steps are you going to take?

APPLICANT: Basically, I need to take my GED classes before I do anything else first.

WORKER: GED classes, you can take those, but still. . . .

APPLICANT: Maybe re-enroll in the Work First Program so I can try to get this license, cosmetologist license, that will help. It's basically because I'm lazy.

WORKER: But why, that's the thing. Why?

APPLICANT: You get used to doing things like that after a while, no push, no edge.

WORKER: You should be pushing yourself, you've got two girls sitting there.

APPLICANT: This might be the wake-up call.

WORKER: You got two girls, I mean if you don't sit up here and make a difference in their lives, you gonna have another generation of young girls getting pregnant early and not finishing school. Or either you going to have a young lady that's going to think, okay, I don't have to do anything and you don't want that. You don't want that. You've got to realize if you do not push them now, you're going to end up with problems that you never thought you'd have. Right now you're saying they're very talented, one likes to sing, one's very active; they have very good skills so far that you see, so push them, but you gotta push yourself too. When they studying you can be studying. And there's nothing out here. Ain't no man.

APPLICANT: I know that.

WORKER: It ain't gonna be no man for when your child gets older. There are no men, okay? You know that as well as I do. You not going to find nobody that's going to come in here, help you out; work, you work, y'all achieve something together. Those days is over with. So this, right now, you're in the Summer Project Program. You have until the program starts in June. They're going to pick you up. It's going to deal with basically the same things that Work First dealt with. Computer training, job skills, on site day care. Right now we're going into May, it starts June, it ends the week before Detroit Public Schools go back. So right now, it will be nice, but if you don't really take an active part the case will be closing. It's not a thing with myself, it's not a thing with Glendale, this is Lansing, all this is Lansing. This is just my sheet, okay? This is Lansing; they want these cases closed and that's why we've been trying to come out, the workers have been trying to come out, this is it. So, if you don't really take an active part now, you can't come back through the door. Governor Engler is leaving in two years. He's going to go out with a bang, okay. He did all these great things and he's going to show it. And he's doing it right now. We've cut the rolls of welfare. What people don't realize is that other states do not have programs like this, they phased them out. Some states don't even pay for day care. Here you get day care assistance, you get job training, take advantage. So, what I'm going to have you do is sign these papers now and you've got until June and while you're at home I want you to really think about what you are going to do to not only help yourself but help those children also. Because, if you're a cosmetologist and you can do hair, you could have had your own business.

APPLICANT: I understand, I been lazy.

WORKER: I know, but we can't sit back and say well, life isn't fair to me, put today's date, 4/26, people haven't helped me and everything. And then we have people who come over here from other countries who just take off. They take advantage of everything and you can't blame them. You can't sit back and say somebody owes us something because the days of welfare are now phasing off and it's not going to be kind to the people that live in the Highland Park Detroit area. They passed a new tax law too. Your landlord could all of a sudden come in and say okay, I'm going to sell the property, what you going to do? There's no place to move. There's no section 8; you can't sign up for that. Section 8 has stopped. Loft in Detroit is $600,000; condos start at $150,000. They are forcing the people in the neighborhood right off 75 and the Boulevard out to put up condos at $220,000. Anytime they take an apartment building here on Seward and turn it into a condominium, and sell a one-bedroom at $60,000 or $90,000, things is changing and if you can go into a service job such as doing hair, make some money, and take care of your family then do it. . . . You gotta do it. So, I'm going to see you in June.

APPLICANT: Okay.

The worker here begins by explicitly asking how much money the applicant has earned doing hair. She then proceeds to rebuke the applicant for not reporting the small amount of income earned from hairstyling, lectures and scolds her about working under the table, and tells the applicant she can be "kicked out" of the TANF program as well as her home for using it as a place of business. Yet there is also an element of coaching and counseling, albeit in a firm and deliberate way, as the worker genuinely tries to get the applicant to better her situation. She tries to encourage the applicant to capitalize on her cosmetology skills and to serve as a positive role model for her two daughters. The worker further conveys the temporary nature of TANF, that it's not she, but rather the state of Michigan, which has become determined to cut people off the rolls. The worker also stresses the importance of education and self-improvement and the power of self-sufficiency.

Demographics of the Clients

Also collected as part of the encounter data was demographic information about the clients included in the sample. Table 6.7 provides data on the race, gender, and language of the TANF clients or applicants. It should be stressed that these data represent a sample of the race, ethnicity, and gender of welfare clients; they are calculated on the basis of observations of client flow in each office. As the data show, the majority of the clients or applicants included in the study sample of these four states are women and African Americans. Additional research might address the issue of representative bureaucracy or the extent to which women and African Americans working at the street level of bureaucracy help women and African American applicants or clients receive TANF benefits.

**Table 6.7. Race, Gender, and Language of
Clients or Applicants Included in Sample.**

Race	%
White	25.0
African American	64.2
Latino	8.8
American Indian	0.0
Asian	0.2
Other	1.9
Gender	
Male	4.8
Female	77.7
Language	
English	80.7
Spanish	2.5
Other (e.g., Arabic)	1.1

Percentages may not total 100 due to missing data.

How Long Do the Encounters Last?

Finally, it is worth noting, as seen in table 6.8, that the average time of
each encounter across all sites is about 40 minutes. Interestingly, however, the range is quite high. Because each welfare applicant or client
presents a unique set of issues or problems, the time involved for each
interview can vary substantially. It may be that workers are treating each
person individually, and not merely as a case or a statistic in the We-
berian sense.[4] This further reflects the discretionary powers of street-
level workers. As Maynard-Moody and Musheno describe it:

> More than bureaucratic politics, identity politics shape the citizen-
> clients' outcomes. The street-level work world is ambiguous and
> marked by conflicting signs, leaving the worker to determine how to
> respond. . . . Street-level workers first establish citizen-clients' identi-
> ties and then respond. Once fixed, these identities shape the nature of
> street-level workers' responses, from bending the rules and providing
> extraordinary assistance to allowing only begrudgingly and minimal
> help and at times to abuse.[5]

Table 6.8. Elapsed Time of Encounters, by State (minutes).

State	Mean	S.D.
Georgia	59.9	43.4
Michigan	42.2	57.4
New York	16.4	20.9
Texas	71.0	53.0
Total	39.7	46.1

The Challenging Job of Street-Level Welfare Workers

The 1996 welfare reform act was intended to change the work of front-line workers in welfare offices. Perhaps it hasn't gone very far in doing so. By and large, workers continue to engage in eligibility determination activities, as compared to employment services or diversion. This was seen in the aggregate by comparing the three goal clusters and through a breakdown of the various topics addressed and activities undertaken by street-level bureaucrats in welfare offices.

This is not to say, of course, that the welfare state has not changed dramatically across the nation. Indeed, if the measure of success was caseload decline, then the reform law was extremely effective. As discussed in chapter 2, caseloads have dropped significantly, and some smaller states (e.g., Wyoming and Idaho) have nearly cleared their caseloads.[6] But, as noted throughout this book, the changes to welfare may be due more to the overall system changes (e.g., requiring work; time limits; creating separate work agencies to provide employment services, etc.) than to the work of the front-line staff in welfare offices. This in no way diminishes the work of street-level bureaucrats, as determining eligibility remains an important task under welfare reform, as it almost certainly will continue to be. In fact, street-level workers represent a critical infrastructure to the welfare system, and the work, to put it mildly, ain't easy.

The workers in welfare offices who have face-to-face contact with welfare applicants and clients have a most exhausting, challenging job. They work with one of the most helpless and vulnerable client popu-

lations of government and, as such, are placed in complex, stressful social situations. They work long hours at low pay, have enormous caseloads, substantial administrative demands (e.g., paperwork), and the
burnout rate is extraordinarily high.[7] A common joke among social
workers goes something like this:

QUESTION: How many social workers does it take to change a light bulb?
ANSWER: I'll do it, but I have 172 other light bulbs to change first.[8]

Despite the challenges faced by front-line staff in social and human
services agencies, there continues to be a supply of people who are
interested in joining the profession of social work. These are people
who are interested in helping the needy or, more generally, have a commitment to the profession and mission of social work.[9] Certainly, some
enter the profession because it is a government job that offers job security. Whatever the motivation, they are, as Maynard-Moody and
Musheno suggest, the "coal miners of policy: they do the hard, dirty
and dangerous work of the state."[10]

Thus, while street-level workers may not be directly responsible for
certain outcomes of welfare reform (e.g., caseload reductions), the system of welfare, which will always exist in some form, could not operate without them.[11]

CHAPTER SEVEN

How Public Management Matters

Public managers have played a crucial role in the implementation of welfare reform in our nation. Their impact has been important at the broad levels of policy and management reform as well as at the level of organization outputs, where managers have effectively created work environments enabling their staff to perform their jobs (e.g., delivering services to the public). Walking a delicate balance between the two conflicting goals of welfare reform, public managers in welfare offices have effectively signaled to workers that both income maintenance and self-sufficiency remain important goals. Indeed, managers have taken important steps to help ensure that the critical task of eligibility determination has remained a key job function of welfare agencies.

There is, however, a level of bureaucratic activity where management has much less of an impact—at the front lines or street level of service delivery. As the research in this book shows, the behaviors and actions of street-level bureaucrats can be explained more by the professional norms, work customs, and occupational culture of the workers than by management factors. This is not due to subversive or insurgent attitudes on the part of street-level workers. Rather, the norms and culture factors represent familiar patterns, methods, and routines—a paradigm, so to speak—to which workers comfortably and sometimes unconsciously revert. Yet front-line workers may be open to management directives, and several suggestions to increase the manageability of street-level bureaucrats were offered in chapter 5. However, even if managers are successful at redirecting some of the behaviors and actions of street-level workers, an eligibility-compliance culture will continue to pervade welfare bureaucracies, as Bane and Elwood predicted.[1]

In effect, as was found in the research presented in this book, street-level bureaucrats, compelled by a professional ethos, will prioritize their activities, allocating most of their time to eligibility determination functions compared with job services. Gais, for example, observes:

> New processes emphasizing work have *not* replaced the older welfare agency orientation that stresses extensive paperwork and documentation to minimize eligibility errors. This agency "culture" persists. . . . Thus, communications between front-line workers [in welfare offices] and clients remain dominated by eligibility processes, which are "hard wired" in the procedures guiding their interactions. The persistence of this eligibility/compliance culture means that communications bottlenecks may occur at the front lines. Earnings disregards, state EITCs [Earned Income Tax Credits], transitional assistance, personal responsibility agreements, and many other services or expectations may not be clearly explained.[2]

The bottom line is that eligibility determination will remain an important goal to the welfare system. And to the extent that street-level workers are driven by their professional norms as well as work customs and ethics that favor helping needy, indigent people receive welfare benefits, this eligibility-compliance culture is unlikely to dissipate.

This raises an important issue that requires further attention: If street-level bureaucrats are driven by work norms and customs, are they remiss in implementing the policies that the state intended to be delivered? As suggested in chapter 4, if the state can't control the bureaucrats, then how can it control the bureaucracy? Perhaps it is the case, as Heclo, Kaufman, and others have told us, that bureaucracies are so entrenched they cannot be readily changed or redirected.[3] Hummel puts it this way: "Citizens and politicians have trouble controlling the runaway bureaucratic machine"—moreover, "Clients can't get the goods from it."[4]

This has major implications, in a broader sense, for democracy and the relationship between the citizen and the state; that is, that which the state expects to be delivered to citizens is not actually being delivered.

While this issue goes well beyond the scope of this book, it certainly merits careful investigation.

Despite the intractability of street-level bureaucrats, the state has been successful in changing the system of welfare. Just how has it done this? What have some of the outcomes of welfare reform been? These issues are addressed in the following sections.

How Management and Welfare Reform Altered the System of Welfare

The 1996 welfare reform law went a long way in changing the welfare system. Perhaps one of the most significant factors in changing the system was the policy of federalism—the devolution of authority over welfare from the federal government to the states. By shifting responsibility to the states, which are clearly unable to handle the fiscal stresses and burdens of large, costly programs as the federal government can, the welfare system was certain—indeed, destined—to evanesce.

Another critical feature of reform was the policy and management decision by state governments to place the responsibility for the delivery of employment services into an organizational unit separate from the income maintenance delivery unit. At some level, state governments recognized that they could not control or redirect the activities of street-level workers, who have historically been responsible for processing people for welfare eligibility—not for jobs. Unable to change the culture of existing welfare bureaucracies, the authorities created separate, distinct bureaucracies, which were charged with delivering work services to welfare clients. Thus, there was an expectation that staff in employment agencies and not in welfare agencies would deliver job services. This sent a clear signal to street-level bureaucrats that the welfare-to-work function would be performed not by them, but by other, more specialized employment counselors. As argued in this book, the decision to separate income maintenance services from employment or work-first services is a very compelling explanation for how the welfare system was reformed. And this factor may help to explain the decline in caseloads.

Although the executive branches of government may have played a more salient role in welfare reform, legislative provisions and requirements at the federal and state levels also contributed to changes in the welfare system.[5] For example, the abolishment of entitlement to aid and the imposition of time limits inevitably changed client behavior. These provisions serve to deter welfare applicants from coming onto the rolls, as well as to kick them off once they have reached their time limits.

The mandatory work participation requirement also serves as a de facto deterrent, even for persons who may otherwise be eligible for welfare benefits. A report by Rockefeller Institute of Government points out:

> Often, families must seek jobs, register with workforce development agencies, look for alternatives to cash assistance, or comply with child support enforcement efforts before qualifying for cash assistance. Employability is determined not by conducting broad assessments, but rather by requiring most people to look for jobs and then letting the labor market determine who is, or who is not, capable of getting and keeping jobs.[6]

And, as illustrated in this book, the signal of "work first" may be getting through to the clients via organizational cues and processes and not necessarily by the street-level workers in welfare agencies. The same Rockefeller Institute report also finds this to be the case:

> The new signals have been expressed most vigorously at the "front door" of state and local welfare systems, [but] through institutional processes rather than clear and detailed explanations from front-line workers.[7]

Gais takes this point even further:

> The importance of work is communicated through new requirements at the "front door" of welfare systems, such as requirements to register

with workforce development or labor bureaucracies; to attend orientations that highlight work and independence goals; to contact employers or otherwise search for work, sometimes before assistance is provided; to comply with other requirements, such as child support enforcement.[8]

Thus, a number of planned and executed managerial, political, and legal mandates fundamentally reformed the welfare state. And there was little that street-level bureaucrats could do to alter this, despite their discretionary powers.

Outcomes of Welfare Reform

As many have argued, the changes to the welfare system as a result of welfare reform have not necessarily been favorable for the population that most relies on and that historically has been most served by welfare—the poor. As Brodkin has pointed out:

> Often, laws produce more smoke than fire, intimating big change, but producing little. Not this time. In ways both apparent and not fully appreciated, welfare reform has reconfigured both the policy and political landscape.[9]

Perhaps most frequently cited as the indicator of welfare reform's success is the dramatic drop in caseloads. Between 1997 and 2001, caseloads dropped by nearly 60 percent. But what has happened to the poor families who comprise that high percentage of caseload reductions? Have they been placed in jobs that have truly resulted in self-sufficiency? Or, have they descended even deeper into poverty? While research to answer these questions is still incomplete and well beyond the research presented in this book, initial readings of the existing evidence are bleak.[10]

Part of the problem here is that reliable data are difficult to acquire. Gais elaborates:

> Although the "front door" of welfare systems has changed substantially, the "back door" has not. Local welfare systems have little contact with

welfare leavers and one result has been low take-up rates of support services for clients who get jobs and leave cash assistance.[11]

One of the early studies on job placement showed that TANF clients who find jobs generally work long hours but are paid low wages. Moreover, the jobs held by parents who have left welfare generally do not provide basic benefits such as paid sick days, vacation leave, or health insurance. Parrot concludes that TANF

> recipients who find jobs are likely to have incomes that are inadequate to meet their families' basic needs. Earnings alone are likely to be particularly inadequate for families in which the parent has very low skills. For many families, a combination of earnings, cash and in-kind government income support, and in the case of single-parents child support from the non-custodial parent will be necessary to make ends meet.[12]

A more recent study conducted by the Institute for Women's Policy Research (IWPR) shows that the conditions or circumstances faced by TANF recipients or leavers have worsened.[13] Relying on longitudinal data from the U.S. Census Bureau's Survey of Income and Program Participation, the IWPR found the following:

- "Although more low-income single parents are working in the wake of welfare reform, well over three-fourths (78 percent) are concentrated in four typically low-wage occupations.

- "Despite increased work participation, no significant increase was found in the share who received health insurance through employment. . . . To the contrary, employed welfare recipients actually experienced a decline in access to employer-provided health insurance (from 21 to 14 percent) after welfare reform.

- "Following welfare reform, poor single-parent families not receiving TANF were more likely to live in dire poverty. This group also slipped deeper into poverty.

- "Low-income, single-mother subfamilies (families who lived in households headed by another) saw their incomes decline following welfare reform (from $664 to 647 per month) as did their participation in

AFDC/TANF (from 27.8 to 14.6 percent), and the proportion receiving food stamps (from 36.8 to 22.1 percent).

- "The educational attainment of single parents declined under the work-first focused policies associated with welfare reform. Of particular concern is the decline in the share of low-income single parents who have some college education, particularly among welfare recipients (from 24.1 to 16.8 percent) following welfare reform. The apparent decreased access to higher education raises questions about the ability of low-income single parents to acquire the skills and credentials they need for long-term success."[14]

Miller found similar results. Relying on a data set consisting of over 30,000 people targeted for welfare-to-work programs over the past decade, she found that

> many families continue to need assistance after they leave welfare. Many families who leave and stay off long term remain poor after they leave, and many lack access to important benefits, such as Food Stamps and health insurance, for which they are probably still eligible. People who leave welfare without work have always been a group of special concern, and the findings indicate that they did not leave welfare without work because they got married. Rather, they were unable to overcome a range of potential barriers to work, such as low education and little prior work experience. These leavers need services to help them find and keep jobs.[15]

The Future of the Welfare State

Evelyn Brodkin, in a provocative and insightful essay titled, "Requiem for Welfare," states the following:

> The demise of the old welfare marked more than an end to a policy that many believed had outlived its usefulness. It also marked the end of welfare politics as we knew it. In the tepid debate over reauthorization in the fall of 2002, the bitter conflicts of earlier years over government's role in addressing poverty were replaced by half-hearted tin-

kering. Even provisions with the potential to induce hand-to-hand combat—such as those on marriage or the superwaiver—elicited relatively low-intensity challenges. Is this because the new welfare yielded the benefits that liberals had hoped for, removing a contentious issue from the table and conferring legitimation on the poor, not as recipients, but as workers? Did it satisfy conservatives by clearing caseloads and demanding work? That does not seem to be the case. If the poor have benefitted from a new legitimacy, it is hard to see the rewards.[16]

As we near the ten-year anniversary of the Personal Responsibility and Work Opportunity Reconciliation Act (PRWORA), the fuller effects of the law will become more apparent. For example, sorely needed outcome data will become more available, thus enabling studies to explore more fully and reliably the relationship between declining caseloads and poverty. There is little doubt even at this point, however, that the welfare state did change dramatically and that further dystopian outcomes are likely once TANF is reauthorized (as of this writing, TANF has not yet undergone reauthorization). If conservatives win the battle, the result will be less funding for cash assistance, welfare-to-work programs, child care, and other services. Moreover, the plans being considered by both houses of Congress ignore the fiscal crises that most states are facing.[17] A recent report issued by the Children's Defense Fund suggests the following:

- **"TANF Funding.** The [Bush] Administration's plan adds no additional dollars to the Temporary Assistance for Needy Families (TANF) block grant. Without an adjustment for inflation over the next five years, the block grant will lose 29 percent of its current value. In FY 2000, States spent about $2 billion more than their annual block grant, by dipping into prior years' funds. States will quickly spend any remaining prior year funds as they try to meet increased work requirements and attempt to fill state budget deficits. In addition, many states [e.g., due to rising unemployment rates] have seen their caseloads increase slightly in recent months.

- "**Work Requirements.** The Bush plan would require that more families work more hours. Under the proposal families would be required to be engaged in a work activity for 40 hours per week. . . . In addition, the Bush Administration would require that states put 70 percent of their caseload in work, or suffer financial consequences. Currently, states have about one-third of their caseload in work.

- "**State Flexibility.** Although the Administration claims that state flexibility lies at the heart of welfare reform, the Bush plan limits state flexibility and tells states how to run their welfare programs. The plan would mandate that states require parents to spend at least 24 hours a week in a very limited set of work activities (unsubsidized employment, work experience, community service or on-the-job training), while allowing them to use other activities (such as job search, GED classes, or vocational education) for the remaining 16 hours of required work.

- "**Child Care Funding.** The Bush budget proposal would provide no new child care funds for the next five years, despite increased work requirements. The Administration plan would allow 114,000 fewer children to receive child care assistance over the next five years. . . . Only one in seven children who are federally eligible for child care assistance receives it. Florida and Texas each have 37,000 families waiting for child care assistance; in Massachusetts the list is 18,000.

- "**Employment and Training.** The Administration says that welfare reform should move families into permanent employment, yet the plan will push states to abandon strategies that help families find higher paying jobs. Under the proposal, job search, vocational education or job skills training directly related to employment do not count towards the first 24 hours of required work in a family's 40-hour work week. The current law allows vocational education (for 12 months maximum), job skills training, and education related to employment to count as a work activity.

- "**Work Supports.** The Administration's proposal makes no efforts to ensure that families moving from welfare-to-work get the benefits—such as food stamps, health care, child care and transportation help—for which they are eligible. Research reveals that many families trading welfare for work do not receive work supports that can help them stay on the job. Those families that have made a successful transition from welfare to work and do receive work supports may be in danger of losing them."

It may be apt to conclude at this point that perhaps the law did "end welfare as we knew it," as Bill Clinton promised. However, it did not fundamentally change the job duties and responsibilities of street-level bureaucrats in welfare agencies. Nor were public managers able or necessarily attempting to shift the job tasks of front-line welfare workers. There will always be some level of social services in need of delivery to various populations in our society. It seems likely that street-level workers can be relied upon to deliver those services.

Appendix A. Survey of TANF Front-Line Practices
Rockefeller Institute of Government

Dear Staff Member,

Thank you for participating in this study on the front-line practices in offices serving TANF (formerly AFDC) clients. The study is being conducted by the Rockefeller Institute of Government in Albany, New York. The survey asks about many aspects of your job and agency, and takes about 15-20 minutes to complete.

We appreciate your cooperation in completing the survey. No one in your agency will know how you answered. You do not need to put your name or identifying information anywhere on this questionnaire, and your answers will remain confidential.

There are no right or wrong answers to our questions. We just want your honest and thoughtful judgments about welfare and your job. Your opinions and perceptions are very useful to our study. We hope you find it interesting.

IF YOU DO NOT MEET FACE-TO-FACE WITH TANF (FORMERLY AFDC) CLIENTS, DO NOT COMPLETE THIS SURVEY. PLEASE CHECK HERE [   ] AND RETURN IT TO THE ROCKEFELLER INSTITUTE RESEARCHER.

1. Program Goals

How important is each of the following goals for your office? Circle the appropriate number.

	Not at all		Somewhat		A great deal	No opinion
A. Reducing the number of people on welfare	1	2	3	4	5	6
B. Determining eligibility for benefits and services accurately	1	2	3	4	5	6
C. Determining eligibility in a timely manner	1	2	3	4	5	6
D. Diverting applicants from going on welfare............................	1	2	3	4	5	6
E. Requiring and/or encouraging work	1	2	3	4	5	6
F. Helping people get the best possible job they can get................	1	2	3	4	5	6
G. Making sure everyone who is eligible receives medical benefits	1	2	3	4	5	6
H. Making sure everyone who is eligible receives child care.....................................	1	2	3	4	5	6
I. Helping people achieve self-sufficiency	1	2	3	4	5	6
J. Preventing fraudulent behavior among clients................................	1	2	3	4	5	6
K. Reducing out-of-wedlock births.....	1	2	3	4	5	6
L. Treating clients fairly and equitably..	1	2	3	4	5	6

Of all the above goals (A-L), which one do you think is most important to your agency?

       (Indicate the letter) _____

Which one do you think is most important to state political officials?   (Indicate the letter) _____

Which one is most important to you in your current position?   (Indicate the letter) _____

2. Staff Training

In any of the past **three years**, have you received training on the items below?
If you answer yes, please indicate whether the training was formal (for example, workshop or classroom training) or informal (for example, on-the-job training or training by your supervisor), or both.

		YES	NO	If YES, circle: Formal	Informal	Both
A.	Informing clients about financial work incentives/earnings disregards	1	2	1	2	3
B.	Granting temporary deferrals or exemptions from work participation requirements	1	2	1	2	3
C.	Informing clients about transitional benefits if they leave welfare for work	1	2	1	2	3
D.	Assessing clients' employability	1	2	1	2	3
E.	Coaching/counseling clients about work	1	2	1	2	3
F.	Sanctioning clients for noncompliance with program rules..........................	1	2	1	2	3
G.	Improving clients' self-esteem	1	2	1	2	3
H.	Monitoring clients' work participation	1	2	1	2	3
I.	Reducing error rates in eligibility or benefits determination....................	1	2	1	2	3
J.	Removing clients' barriers to employment	1	2	1	2	3
K.	Verifying information provided by clients in order to prevent fraud	1	2	1	2	3
L.	Monitoring clients' time clocks under welfare	1	2	1	2	3
M.	Granting extensions of or exemptions from welfare time limits	1	2	1	2	3
N.	Treating clients fairly and equitably	1	2	1	2	3

3. Supervision

We would like to learn more about how your performance in various aspects of your job is monitored by your supervisor or other managers in your office.
For each of the areas of job responsibility please circle the appropriate response.

Job Responsibility	This is NOT part of my job.	If this IS part of your job, please circle a number below:	
		My performance on this is NOT monitored or is monitored informally.	My performance on this IS monitored and/or tracked formally.
A. Reducing the number of people on welfare	1	2	3
B. Determining eligibility for benefits and services accurately	1	2	3
C. Determining eligibility in a timely manner	1	2	3
D. Diverting applicants from going on welfare	1	2	3
E. Requiring and/or encouraging work	1	2	3
F. Helping people get the best possible job they can get	1	2	3
G. Making sure everyone who is eligible receives medical benefits	1	2	3
H. Making sure everyone who is eligible receives child care	1	2	3
I. Helping people achieve self-sufficiency	1	2	3
J. Preventing fraudulent behavior among clients	1	2	3
K. Reducing out-of-wedlock births	1	2	3
L. Treating clients fairly and equitably	1	2	3

4. Rules and Judgment

In some areas, staff have clear-cut guidelines or rules about implementing the TANF program, while in others, they need to use their professional judgment. In the following areas, to what extent are decisions based on agency rules and to what extent are they based on staff judgment?

	Always based on clear rules	Usually based on clear rules	Sometimes rules/ sometimes judgment	Usually based on staff judgment	Always based on staff judgment	Don't know	Not my area of responsibility
A. Type of work program or activity welfare client should be assigned to initially	1	2	3	4	5	6	7
B. Type of work program or activity welfare client should be assigned to after job search	1	2	3	4	5	6	7
C. Diverting applicants from applying for welfare benefits	1	2	3	4	5	6	7
D. When to temporarily defer client from work participation requirements	1	2	3	4	5	6	7
E. When to exempt client from work participation requirements	1	2	3	4	5	6	7
F. When to sanction a client	1	2	3	4	5	6	7
G. When to remove a sanction	1	2	3	4	5	6	7
H. How to handle Food Stamps when applicant is ineligible for cash assistance ...	1	2	3	4	5	6	7
I. How to handle Medicaid when applicant is ineligible for cash assistance ...	1	2	3	4	5	6	7
J. When to authorize child care	1	2	3	4	5	6	7

5. Management/Leadership Practices

Please answer the following questions based on your direct supervisor.

A. During the past three years, how often has your supervisor discussed the goals of welfare reform with you?

    1   2   3   4
  Never   Rarely   Occasionally   Often

B. To what extent is your unit organized with an eye toward reaching these goals?

    1   2   3   4   5
 Not at all   Somewhat   A great deal

C. Does your supervisor hold regularly scheduled staff meetings?   ❑ 1. Yes   ❑ 2. No (Go to E.)

D. How often?   ❑ 1. about once a week

              ❑ 2. about once every 2 weeks

              ❑ 3. about once a month

              ❑ 4. less than once a month

E. Not counting regular meetings, does your supervisor hold staff meetings as they are needed?   ❑ 1. Yes   ❑ 2. No

F. How free do workers feel to raise issues and problems at staff meetings (e.g., to air grievances, discuss problems, have input into administrative or other critical decisions, etc.)?

    1   2   3   4   5
 Not at all   Somewhat   A great deal

G. How would you describe worker morale in your office?

    1   2   3   4   5
 Very low   Fair   Very high

H. All things considered, how satisfied are you with your current job?

    1   2   3   4   5
 Not at all   Neutral   Very
 satisfied   satisfied

I. There are different styles of decision-making in organizations that range from very centralized (i.e., where the decisions are made only by supervisors and the higher-ups; it is very hierarchical) to very decentralized (i.e., where front-line workers such as yourself participate in various types of decisions).

In general, how would you describe the decision-making structure of your office:

    1   2   3   4   5
 Centralized   Decentralized

J. General communication and management style differ from office to office.
Based on your office, please answer the following questions:

	Not At All		Somewhat		Very	No Opinion
a. How open is communication between you and your supervisor?	1	2	3	4	5	6
b. How good is lateral communication where you have the opportunity to share information and knowledge with co-workers?	1	2	3	4	5	6
c. How good is the communication of information downward (from office managers to supervisors to you)?	1	2	3	4	5	6
d. How loyal is your supervisor to staff?	1	2	3	4	5	6
e. How innovative and creative is your supervisor?	1	2	3	4	5	6

6. Opinions About Welfare

Please describe your views about welfare.

	Strongly Disagree		Neutral		Strongly Agree	No Opinion
A. Everyone can get off welfare if they want	1	2	3	4	5	6
B. People can get a job if they want	1	2	3	4	5	6
C. It is fair to require welfare recipients to work	1	2	3	4	5	6
D. It is better for children under age 3 to be home with their parent(s) than to be in day care	1	2	3	4	5	6
E. Time limits will be the most effective way to get people off of welfare	1	2	3	4	5	6

		Strongly Disagree		Neutral		Strongly agree	No opinion
F.	Welfare time limits are a fair policy....................................	1	2	3	4	5	6
G.	My office provides a lot of help and support to clients who really want to get off of welfare...............	1	2	3	4	5	6
H.	It is very easy for clients to stay on welfare and make little or no effort to get off	1	2	3	4	5	6
I.	The economic situation in my county makes it easy for welfare recipients to find a job	1	2	3	4	5	6
J.	It is easy for welfare recipients in my county to find a job that pays enough to support themselves and their children..........	1	2	3	4	5	6
K.	Time limits are not permanent; they will be eliminated in a few years	1	2	3	4	5	6

7. Views of Clients

When you think about TANF recipients, approximately how many:

		Percentage of Recipients						
		0%	1-24%	25-49%	50%	51-75%	76-99%	100%
A.	would rather be on welfare than work to support their family?	1	2	3	4	5	6	7
B.	believe the time limit will not be enforced?	1	2	3	4	5	6	7
C.	feel bad about themselves because they are on welfare?.............................	1	2	3	4	5	6	7
D.	would feel better about themselves if they had a job?	1	2	3	4	5	6	7
E.	believe it is fair that the welfare system requires them to work?	1	2	3	4	5	6	7
F.	receive welfare due to circumstances beyond their control	1	2	3	4	5	6	7

8. Your Personal Characteristics

A. What is your job title? _____

B. How long have you been in your current position? _____ years _____ months

C. How long have you worked with welfare clients? _____ years _____ months

D. Have you ever received welfare benefits? ☐ 1. Yes ☐ 2. No

E. Which of the following responsibilities do you have in your job?
(Please check as many as applicable.)

    ☐ a. Briefly helping, checking, or collecting information from clients at
the reception desk or nearby

    ☐ b. Determining and redetermining eligibility for cash assistance through TANF
(formerly AFDC)

    ☐ c. Determining and redetermining eligibility for Food Stamps or Medicaid

    ☐ d. Preparing people for employment, helping them search for jobs, or
referring them to jobs

    ☐ e. Determining and redetermining eligibility for child care services and/or
authorizing payment for child care

    ☐ f. None of the above

G. Of your total work time last week, please estimate what percentage of your time was spent in direct
contact with TANF clients in person or by phone.

    _____ %

G. What is your gender? ☐ 1. Male ☐ 2. Female

H. What is your race or ethnic background? ☐   1. White (not hispanic)

                                              ☐   2. African American (not hispanic)

                                              ☐   3. Latino/Hispanic (regardless of race)

                                              ☐   4. American Indian

                                              ☐   5. Asian or Pacific Islander

                                              ☐   6. Other

I. What is the highest grade or level in school or college that you have completed?

    ☐ 1. GED
    ☐ 2. High School Diploma
    ☐ 3. Some college
    ☐ 4. Associate's degree (in what area _____)
    ☐ 5. Bachelor's degree (in what area _____)
    ☐ 6. Some graduate work (in what area _____)
    ☐ 7. Master's degree or higher (in what area _____)

Appendix B. Data and Data Collection

As noted in chapter 1, there were four primary sources of data for this study: (1) content review of agency documents, (2) face-to-face semi-structured interviews, (3) paper-and-pencil surveys, and (4) direct observations of "encounters."

Content reviews of agency documents provided information on agency and office hierarchies, formal agency policy and goal statements, personnel systems, management information systems, and client intake systems.

The semi-structured interviews with high-level agency officials, managers, and supervisors were intended to capture information about program characteristics, management practices, human resource practices, management information systems, interorganizational structures, program activities, and local understanding of policy and operative goals. Anywhere from two to six administrators, managers, and supervisors were interviewed in each site, as well as two to ten front-line workers.

The on-site surveys were administered to all workers who had face-to-face contact or interaction with welfare applicants or clients in the welfare agencies. The survey asked staff questions about their understanding of the primary program goals for their office, their receipt of training in the prior three years, the extent of supervision and performance rewards, the extent of professional judgment they were expected to exercise in their work with clients, their assessment of the agency's management and leadership practices, their personal opinions about welfare and clients, and their demographic and professional characteristics.

A total of 286 surveys were administered to the front-line workers in welfare offices, including receptionists, benefit eligibility specialists, employment counselors, specialized case workers, and others who provided welfare, child care, or employment-related services. A total of 200 surveys were returned for a 70 percent response rate overall (see chapter 5). The larger version of this study also examined the employment offices in each site responsible for welfare-to-work goals. However, given the small number of workers sampled in these agencies and the greater clarity of the goals of these agencies and workers, only front-line staff in the welfare offices are included in this study.

Finally, the direct observations or encounters provide data on the actual content and process of front-line practices in welfare offices. To collect a representative sample of these encounters, a quota sample was developed based on the amount of time workers spent in face-to-face contact with TANF clients or applicants. The sample was constructed on the basis of "time," because time spent by front-line workers in face-to-face encounters represented the most comparable analysis unit across sites and organizations. Thus, the sampling unit was defined as "minutes of time workers spend in face-to-face encounters" with TANF applicants or clients per week. Based on surveys of front-line staff in the sampling frame, the average "encounter time" for staff was computed. Hours were then computed to percentages of the entire, weekly "encounter time" at each site. A stratified quota sample for observation (sixty hours per site) was then allocated across sites in proportion to the share of the total site encounter time. After determining the quota of hours to be observed within each unit of the site, individual front-line workers within each unit were randomly selected for observation. These workers were observed for a minimum three and a maximum of six hours, until the quota of observation hours for the unit was reached.

To collect sufficiently detailed information, the encounters were either tape-recorded (permission was granted for the sites in Texas and Michigan) or transcribed verbatim (New York and Georgia sites). A total of 730 encounters in welfare offices were observed for this study. This includes one-on-one conversations as well as unscheduled streams of clients. This qualitative data set represents an empirical milestone for research on street-level bureaucrats in that the interviews between street-level bureaucrats and welfare clients capture the actual *behaviors* of street-level workers.

The encounter data were classified into "topic," "purpose," or "activity" categories. "Topic" refers to the topics covered or discussed in the encounter (e.g., food stamps, Medicaid, employment, time limits, participation); "purpose" is the primary purpose of the encounter (e.g., application for TANF, food stamps, or Medicaid; application for child care; suspected fraud), and "activity" refers to either the actions of the front-line worker (e.g., collecting information, explaining options, assessing employment) or the actions of the client (e.g., inquiring about rules or benefits). Inter-rater reliability tests were conducted to ensure sufficient reliability of the final codes included in each of the three categories. The inter-rater reliability tests resulted in several codes being dropped from the analysis. The qualitative data analysis program ATLAS was employed to analyze these data. Appendix E provides a full listing of the codes included in each of these categories.

Appendix C. Critical Events Leading to Passage of Welfare Reform

1993

January 20   President Clinton is inaugurated. He promised to "end welfare as we know it" during his presidential campaign.

January 21   U.S. Senator Daniel Patrick Moynihan (D-N.Y.) reintroduces the Work for Welfare Act, which would provide full federal funding for the Job Opportunities and Basic Skills Training Program (JOBS).

February 2   House Ways and Means Committee Republicans introduce a welfare reform bill with two tiers of AFDC, the transition program and the work program. After a total of five years' participation by clients in both programs, states could opt to drop clients from the rolls of Aid to Families with Dependent Children (AFDC).

June 21   The Clinton administration names a 27-member task force to develop a welfare reform plan. The effort is led by Bruce Reed, deputy assistant to the president for domestic policy; David T. Ellwood, assistant secretary for planning and evaluation, U.S. Department of Health and Human Services (HHS); and Mary Jo Bane, HHS assistant secretary, Administration for Children and Families.

November 10   House Republicans unveil H.R. 3500, a welfare reform proposal sponsored by Minority Leader Robert H. Michel (R-Ill.) and cosponsored by 160 Republican lawmakers. The proposal requires that by 2002, 90 percent of those who receive AFDC for two years or more would work in exchange for their benefits. The proposal allows states to convert AFDC to block grants, requires paternity establishment in exchange for AFDC benefits, and denies AFDC to minor parents under age 18. It would save $19.5 billion over five years.

1994

January 25   Sixteen Senate Republicans, including U.S. Senators Bob Dole (Kan.) and Hank Brown (Colo.), introduce the Welfare Reform Act of 1994, S. 1795. It gives states the option of ending AFDC after two years, requires teen mothers to live at home, preserves the AFDC entitlement, and allows for the establishment of a voucher program in which the combined value of AFDC and food stamp benefits can be used as a wage subsidy.

April 15	U.S. Senators Tom Harkin (D-Iowa) and Christopher Bond (R-Mo.) introduce the first bipartisan welfare bill, the Welfare to Self-Sufficiency Act, S. 2009. The bill is modeled after Iowa's Promise Jobs Program.
June 14	President Clinton unveils the Work and Responsibility Act in Kansas City, Missouri.
June 24	The Clinton welfare bill is officially introduced in the Senate as S. 2224 and the House of Representatives as H.R. 4605.
July 29	The House Ways and Means Subcommittee on Human Resources holds hearing on the Clinton welfare reform bill.
November 8	Republicans win a majority in both houses of Congress. The new congressional leaders promise to bring a Contract With America to the House and Senate floors within 100 days. The contract includes the Personal Responsibility Act, which proposes to reform welfare by curbing out-of-wedlock births through denial of benefits. The legislation also imposes a work requirement and caps spending growth of welfare programs. The bill requires all families to be off of AFDC after a total of five years of benefits. It is the first proposal to remove entitlement status from AFDC, SSI, and a number of nutrition programs.

1995

January 5	The House Ways and Means Committee begins hearings on "Contract With America" items, including welfare reform.
March 8	The House Ways and Means Committee approves, 22-11, a welfare reform bill—the Personal Responsibility Act—that would modify 40 federal programs, end the entitlement status of AFDC, and give states considerably more control over public assistance through block grants. The Senate Finance Committee begins hearings on welfare reform.
March 21	The House opens debate on the Personal Responsibility Act.
March 22	The Congressional Budget Office estimates that, although the Personal Responsibility Act will save $66 billion over five years, all 50 states will fail to meet its job requirements.
March 24	The House votes 234-199 to approve H.R. 4, the Personal Responsibility Act. Only nine Democrats supported the measure; five Republicans voted against it.
March 25	President Clinton denounces major elements of the House-passed welfare bill in his weekly radio address.
May 18	Sen. Daniel Patrick Moynihan (D-N.Y.) introduces his welfare reform bill, the Family Support Act of 1995, which retains the individual entitlement status for low-income families.
May 26	The Senate Finance Committee approves, 12-8, a welfare reform proposal from Sen. Bob Packwood (R-Ore.) that would provide $16.7 billion in block grants to the states for temporary assistance to needy families. Similar to the House bill, it includes a $1.7 billion loan fund to states, a five-year lifetime time limit on assistance, and a state option to deny assistance to noncitizens.

September 7	The Senate votes 54-45 to defeat the Democrats' welfare reform plan. The bill would have preserved the entitlement to welfare while increasing the number of recipients enrolled in education, training, and work.
September 19	Following a week of debate, the Senate votes 87-12 to pass the Welfare Reform Act. Senators approve over 40 amendments to the bill, including a compromise leadership amendment, before final passage. The estimated savings is $67 billion over seven years.
October 24	Over 40 House and Senate welfare reform conferees convene to begin working out the differences between the House and Senate bills.
November 8	An analysis of the Senate welfare reform bill by the Office of Management and Budget finds that proposed policy changes would result in one million more children living in poverty.
December 21	The House votes 245-178 to pass the welfare reform conference report.
December 22	The Senate votes 52-47 to pass the conference report. The estimated savings is $58 billion over seven years.

1996

January 9	President Clinton vetoes H.R. 4, the welfare reform conference committee bill. He says that an acceptable welfare reform bill must include more funding for child care, health coverage for low-income families, requirements for state funding, and additional funding during times of economic downturn or population growth.
February 6	The National Governors' Association unanimously approves bipartisan agreements on welfare and Medicaid reform at their winter meeting in Washington, D.C. Both House Speaker Newt Gingrich (R-Ga.) and Senate Majority Leader Bob Dole (R-Kan.) pledge that both houses of Congress will give the governors' policy statements serious consideration.
February 28	HHS Secretary Donna Shalala, testifying before the Senate Finance Committee, announces that the president cannot support the NGA welfare proposal "in its current form." She says that the proposal needs to be modified to provide vouchers for children of parents terminated from assistance, to retain the entitlement status of child welfare services and food stamps, and to include fundamental revision of the immigration section.
March 5	President Clinton notes in a speech before the National Association of Counties that his administration has approved waivers for 53 different welfare reform projects in 37 states, covering nearly 75 percent of all welfare recipients.
April 26	The White House proposes a new welfare reform bill with estimated savings of $38 billion over seven years. HHS Assistant Secretary Mary Jo Bane tells Congress the bill "promotes work, encourages parental responsibility, and provides a safety net for children."
May 18	President Clinton announces his support for a Wisconsin proposal for welfare reform, Wisconsin Works (or W-2), that would end the guarantee of welfare benefits and would require work.

May 22	Congressional Republicans introduce revised welfare reform bills in both the House and Senate that are modeled, in part, on the NGA policy statements. The legislation retains federal control of child protection and adoption programs and allows legal immigrants who are not yet citizens to be eligible for cash welfare. Republicans say they will attach to the welfare bill a plan to give states control of Medicaid.
June 6	The House votes 289-136 to approve H.R. 3562, the Wisconsin Only bill, which would authorize the state of Wisconsin to implement its statewide welfare reform demonstration project, Wisconsin Works.
June 26	Senate Finance Committee approves S. 1795, the Personal Responsibility and Work Opportunity Act of 1996, the Senate Republican leadership's welfare and Medicaid reform legislation.
July 11	House and Senate Republican leadership announce their decision to split the welfare and Medicaid reform bills contained in H.R. 3507 and S. 1795. President Clinton had threatened to veto the reform bill, objecting to the Medicaid provisions.
July 18	The House of Representatives passes, by a vote of 256 to 170, its budget reconciliation package, H.R. 3734, which contains a modified version of the Personal Responsibility and Work Opportunity Act of 1996, H.R. 3507.
July 23	The Senate passes its welfare reform bill by a vote of 74 to 24.
July 25	House and Senate conferees begin meeting to work out the differences between their respective welfare reform measures.
July 30	House-Senate conferees complete work on H.R. 3734 and send the bill to the House for final passage.
July 31	President Clinton announces he will sign H.R. 3734. House of Representatives passes the bill by a vote of 328 to 101.
August 1	Senates passes H.R. 3734 by a vote of 78 to 21.
August 22	President Clinton signs the Personal Responsibility and Work Opportunity Reconciliation Act of 1996.
September 11	Mary Jo Bane, assistant secretary for HHS' Administration for Children and Families, and Peter B. Edelman, acting assistant secretary for HHS Planning and Evaluation, resign, citing concerns about the new welfare reform law.
October 1	Deadline for states to file their plans to opt into the TANF Block Grant. Twenty-three states submit plans; two states, Wisconsin and Michigan, were authorized on September 30 to begin their TANF program.
October 11	Twenty-six states file TANF state plans. The Red Cliff Tribe of Wisconsin becomes the first Native American tribe to file their own TANF plan. Florida is the third state to receive HHS approval for its TANF plan.

Source: American Public Human Services Association, www.aphsa.org/Policy /HistoryWelfare.asp. Date accessed: July 9, 2004.

Appendix D. Chronology of Major Welfare Policy and Legislation Enacted in the United States

1935	Congress passed the Social Security Act, which created Aid to Dependent Children to provide federal funds to needy children and their families.
1939	Related federal activities in the fields of health, education, social insurance, and human services were brought together under the new Federal Security Agency.
1946	The Communicable Disease Center was established, forerunner of the Centers for Disease Control and Prevention. The Cabinet-level Department of Health, Education and Welfare, was created under President Eisenhower, officially coming into existence April 11, 1953. In 1979, the Department of Education Organization Act was signed into law, providing for a separate Department of Education. HEW became the Department of Health and Human Services, officially arriving on May 4, 1980.
1961	First White House Conference on Aging.
1965	The Medicare and Medicaid programs are created, making comprehensive health care available to millions of Americans. The Older Americans Act creates the nutritional and social programs run by HHS' Administration on Aging. The Head Start program created.
1975	Child Support Enforcement program established.
1977	Creation of the Health Care Financing Administration to manage Medicare and Medicaid separately from the Social Security Administration.
1980	Federal funding provided to states for foster care and adoption assistance.
1988	Creation of the JOBS program and federal support for child care initiated. The McKinney Act signed into law, providing health care to the homeless.
1989	Creation of the Agency for Health Care Policy and Research (now Agency for Healthcare Research and Quality).
1993	The Vaccines for Children Program is established, providing free immunizations to all children in low-income families.
1995	The Social Security Administration becomes an independent agency March 31, 1995.
1996	Enactment of welfare reform under the Personal Responsibility and Work Opportunity Reconciliation Act (PRWORA). A num-

	ber of categorical child care entitlements that had been linked to AFDC are consolidated into a single child care development block grant (CCDBG). Like welfare, child care is no longer an entitlement for poor families.
1997	The State Children's Health Insurance Program is established.
1999	The Ticket to Work and Work Incentives Improvement Act of 1999 is signed, making it possible for millions of Americans with disabilities to join the workforce without fear of losing their Medicaid and Medicare coverage. It also modernizes the employment services system for people with disabilities.
2001	The Centers for Medicare & Medicaid Services is created, replacing the Health Care Financing Administration.

Source: U.S. Department of Health and Human Services, www.hhs.gov/about/hhshist.html. Date accessed: June 1, 2003.

Appendix E. Codes for Encounters

TOPIC CODES AND DESCRIPTIONS

CODE	TOPIC: WHAT WORKER IS DISCUSSING

Specific Programs:

food stamps	food stamps (including expedited food stamps)
Medicaid	Medicaid (local terms may be different, e.g., "medical"), transitional Medicaid after leaving welfare for work, Medicaid for children only/children's health insurance program (CHIP)
child care	child care use, child care providers, child care reliability, child care costs/payments/reimbursements, transitional child care after leaving welfare for work, child care for low-income families not on welfare
emergency assistance	emergency cash assistance provided through the welfare office
one-time diversion assistance	one-time diversion assistance; may be cash or a one-time payment for a specific item like car repairs
transportation	client transportation, including car ownership/reliability, value of car, rides from other people, public transportation, gasoline, car repairs, driver's license, car insurance, traffic tickets, etc.
earned income credit	Earned Income Tax Credit (EITC) reduces income taxes for people with earnings
other government services	unemployment insurance (UI), Supplemental Security Income (SSI), Social Security, Home Energy Assistance Program (HEAP), housing programs (e.g., public housing, Section 8, emergency housing assistance), veterans benefits, foster care, child protective services, etc.
community services	food banks, homeless shelters, hospitals and health clinics, family planning clinics, budgeting classes, discounts to low-income customers by gas, electric, and telephone companies, etc.

143

Specific Policies:

absent parent	identity, location, circumstances, etc., of nonresident parents; does not include discussions of child support enforcement
child support enforcement	child support orders, paternity establishment, collections, including reporting of same to welfare office, pass-through of collections to the family, appointments with child support enforcement officers, problems
participation	client's participation in mandatory education/employment activity (work requirement), substance abuse program, or other mandated activity; failure to participate without good cause results in a sanction; participation rules apply to parents but not to other caretakers like grandparents
sanctions	reduction in benefits for failure to comply with program rules without good cause
earnings disregards	a share of earnings are not counted in determining the welfare grant
entitlement	welfare is no longer an entitlement or right; client is expected to become self-sufficient (i.e., off welfare)
benefits without TANF	reference to the availability of food stamps, Medicaid, and/or child care for people who leave TANF or who never come onto TANF; also code the program being discussed (e.g., food stamps, medicaid, or child care)
time limits	limit on the months of welfare payments
PRA	Personal Responsibility Agreement contract
school attendance of children	explaining rules and/or monitoring of children's school enrollment and attendance
immunization of children	explaining rules and monitoring of children's immunization status, shot records
family cap	a family's welfare benefit is not increased with the birth of an additional child
marriage	discussion or activity that appears to promote marriage and the formation of two-parent families
fraud	accusation or investigation of possible client fraud, referral of the case to the agency's fraud unit, references to finger-imaging

Client's Education/Employment:

education (past, current, or future)	education, including high school, adult education, GED programs, college

employment (past, current, or future)	regular paid work
training (past, current, or future)	vocational and other training programs
work experience (past, current, or future)	unpaid work activities, including workfare, work experience, and community service
job readiness/job search (past, current, or future)	orientation, job readiness activities, job search, and job placement
education/employment unclear (past, current, or future)	one of the above education/employment activities but unclear which one

Other Topics:

housing and utilities	client housing problems, including problems with rent, mortgage payments, utilities, housing quality, landlord, etc. Does not include who lives with client and dollar amounts unless these raise problems.
health insurance	health insurance; does not include Medicaid, Medicare, veterans programs, and private health insurance
health, disability, and mental health—client	health status, health problems, disabilities of client
health, disability, and mental health—others	health status, health problems, disabilities of spouse, partner or children
substance abuse	drug or alcohol use, problems, treatments of clients or other family members
pregnancy	pregnancy of client or family member, prenatal care
family planning	additional children, birth control use, family planning services
parenting	client's problems with child's behavior, parent/child interactions, parents as role models
family problems	client's problems with spouse/current or former partner, domestic violence, relationship problems with other family members
crime	problems raised by crime, such as family members in prison, stolen property, etc.

Source: Rockefeller Institute of Government, Albany, New York, Front-Line Management Study.

ACTIVITY CODES AND DESCRIPTIONS

WORKER ACTIVITY CODES	WHAT WORKER IS DOING
Advising:	
collecting info—intentions	asking the client about his or her intentions, plans, or expectations
collecting info—needs	asking the client about needs other than cash assistance, such as Medicaid, food stamps, child care, transportation, other services
explaining options	describing alternative activities, programs, providers, and courses of action available to the client and asking client about preferences
invoking personal beliefs	invoking personal beliefs, values, and experience to advise and counsel client
translating rules/benefits	advising based on interpretations of agency rules, available benefits, and rule-based consequences; explaining a rule in light of the client's particular circumstances, activities, or needs
using professional expertise	using professional expertise, training, and experience to advise and counsel client and/or to attempt to resolve immediate problems
Assessing:	
employment	assessing the client's vocational abilities, interests, and preferences by asking questions, administering a test, asking client to fill out a form or questionnaire, discussing educational or vocational interests
services	assessing the client's needs for services such as child care, transportation, substance abuse programs, mental health services, and housing
Collecting Documents	collecting documents verifying information about a topic listed above
Collecting Information about Circumstances	asking questions about the client's situation or actions regarding a topic listed above, other than monitoring attendance/participation at mandatory activities
Completing or Signing Forms	asking client to fill in and/or sign form, with or without explanation of what is in form or reading form to client

Excepting or Exempting	telling the client an exception or exemption is being made in this case; postponing enforcement of a rule
Explaining Rules	explaining rules, requirements, benefits, services, application procedures, other procedures, and how the process works
MIS Verification	using computer systems and finger-imaging to collect, cross-check, or verify information about the client, either on the spot or with computer-generated reports; including use of computer systems to monitor attendance/participation, references to problems with computer systems

Negative Consequences:

acting on sanctions	referring or explicitly not referring client to the conciliation/sanctioning process; authorizing or explicitly not authorizing a sanction; explaining how client can lift sanction or lifting a sanction
denying benefit	denying cash assistance, other benefits, services
explaining consequences	explaining consequences for failure to comply with rules and procedures; warning that benefits can be denied or reduced for failure to comply
sending for investigation	sending the client or the client's case to be investigated or pursued by a fraud unit, child protective services, child support enforcement

Providing Employment Services:

job placement	referring client to a specific employer with a possible job opening
job readiness/ job search	preparing the client to search for work and assist in job search
Sending to Mandatory Activity	sending or referring client to another person or organization to apply for or receive assistance, engage in activity, receive an assessment, or pursue another activity; client is told he or she must go to secure or keep benefits

Verifying:

contacting for verification	contacting or phoning a landlord, employer, school, or other person or institution to verify information about a topic listed above, or telling client this will be done
monitoring via client	asking the client whether and/or when he or she attended or participated in a mandatory activity

monitoring via   informing the client that the worker has information
  outside source   about attendance/participation from an outside source,
                            such as attendance rosters, phone call from service
                            provider, employer, computer system

sending for verification   sending the client somewhere or to someone to get ver-
                            ification of information about anything, even if the
                            quotation has no topic code

verifying via client   asking for and/or getting from the client information
                            verifying attendance/participation, such as a letter or
                            form

Source: Rockefeller Institute of Government, Albany, N.Y., Front-Line Management Study.

CLIENT

ACTIVITY CODE	WHAT CLIENT IS DOING
Disclosing Problems	disclosing specific problems facing the client, other than a lack of income
Requesting Other Assistance or Service	requesting assistance other than TANF, food stamps, Medicaid, child care, or other government assistance
Declining Benefits	declining, rejecting, or withdrawing from a program, service, work activity, or employment; declining or refusing to provide information or documents; declining to pursue child support; refusing to comply with a rule
Inquiring about Rules or Benefits	
Inquiring about Rights	
Underground Economy	disclosing work or income that is not reported for income tax purposes

Source: Rockefeller Institute of Government, Albany, N.Y., Front-Line Management Study.

PRIMARY PURPOSE CODES AND DESCRIPTIONS

CODE	PRIMARY PURPOSE OF THE ENCOUNTER

The code or codes that most closely describe the primary purpose of the encounter as recorded by the observer.

Select one or more:

application for TANF, FS, or MA	client is applying for one or more of these benefits; may already receive one or more of them. (Note: Because there may be several steps in the application process, this may not be the client's first visit.)
application for child care	client is applying for child care financing or assistance in locating providers
application for other assistance	client is applying for government assistance other than TANF, FS, MA, or child care
other client-initiated visit	client has initiated the visit to address a problem or request help other than applying for government assistance
assessment	client is participating in individual employment assessment or employment counseling; planning for job readiness/job search, employment, education, training, etc.; or receiving an assessment for health, disability, substance abuse, domestic violence, etc.
monitoring	client is being monitored for participation in mandatory activities (education, employment, substance abuse program, etc.) and meeting of other mandates (e.g., child's school attendance, immunization)
attendance problems/ conciliation/ sanctioning	client may have failed to comply with a mandate or other rule
suspected fraud	client is being investigated for possible fraud in applying for or receiving assistance; include preliminary investigations (e.g., FEDS interviews)
attending job readiness/ job search	client is attending job readiness/job search training or receiving individual job search assistance or job placement
recertification/exit interview	client is visiting agency for a periodic recertification of eligibility for assistance; an interview before leaving welfare voluntarily
other	client is in the office for a clear reason, but it is not listed above
purpose unclear	reason for encounter is unclear

Source: Rockefeller Institute of Government, Albany, N.Y., Front-Line Management Study.

Notes

Chapter 1. How Can Management Not Matter?

1. While the author recognizes that some scholars treat "management" and "leadership" as separate concepts, no such distinctions are made here. See, for example, Kenneth J. Meier and Laurence J. O'Toole Jr., "Managerial Strategies and Behavior in Networks: A Model with Evidence from U.S. Public Education," *Journal of Public Administration Research and Theory* 11 (2001): 271–93, and Hal G. Rainey, *Understanding and Managing Public Organizations* (San Francisco: Jossey-Bass, 1997).

2. See, for example, Rainey, *Understanding and Managing*; Patricia W. Ingraham, Philip G. Joyce, and Amy Kneedler Donahue, *Government Performance: Why Management Matters* (Baltimore: Johns Hopkins University Press, 2003); Jerrell D. Coggburn and Saundra K. Schneider, "The Quality of Management and Government Performance: An Empirical Analysis of the American States," *Public Administration Review* 63 (2003): 206–13; Meier and O'Toole, "Managerial Strategies"; Kenneth J. Meier and Laurence J. O'Toole Jr., "Public Management and Organizational Performance: The Effect of Managerial Quality," *Journal of Public Administration Research and Theory* 12 (2002): 629–43; H. George Frederickson and Kevin B. Smith, *The Public Administration Theory Primer* (Boulder, CO: Westview Press, 2003); Laurence J. O'Toole Jr. and Kenneth J. Meier, "Networks, Hierarchies, and Public Management: Modeling and Nonlinearities," in Carolyn Heinrich and Laurence E. Lynn Jr. (eds.), *Governance and Performance: New Perspectives* (Washington, D.C.: Georgetown University Press, 2000); Jeffrey L. Brudney, Laurence J. O'Toole Jr., and Hal G. Rainey, *Advancing Public Management: New Developments in Theory, Methods, and Practice* (Washington, D.C.: Georgetown University Press, 2000); Carolyn J. Heinrich and Laurence E. Lynn Jr., "Government and Performance: The Influence of Programs Structure and Management on Job Training Partnership Act (JTPA) Program Outcomes," in Carolyn Heinrich and Laurence E. Lynn Jr. (eds.), *Governance and Performance: New Perspectives* (Washington, D.C.: Georgetown University Press, 2000); Robert D. Behn, "What Right Do Public Managers Have to Lead?" *Public Administration Review* 58 (May/June 1998): 209–25; Robert D. Behn, "Creating an Inno-

vative Organization: Ten Hints for Involving Frontline Workers," *State and Local Government Review* 27 (1995): 221–34; Robert D. Behn, *Leadership Counts* (Cambridge: Harvard University Press, 1991); Patricia W. Ingraham, James R. Thompson, and Ronald P. Sanders, *Transforming Government* (San Francisco: Jossey-Bass Publishers, 1998); Rainey, *Understanding and Managing*; Donald F. Kettl, "The Global Revolution in Public Management: Driving Themes, Missing Links," *Journal of Policy Analysis and Management* 16 (1997): 446–62; Mark Moore, *Creating Public Value* (Cambridge: Harvard University Press, 1997); Norma M. Riccucci, *Unsung Heroes: Federal Execucrats Making a Difference* (Washington, D.C.: Georgetown University Press, 1996); Larry D. Terry, *Leadership of Public Bureaucracies: The Administrator as Conservator* (Thousand Oaks, CA: Sage Publications, 1995); Robert B. Denhardt, *The Pursuit of Significance: Strategies for Managerial Success in Public Organizations* (Belmont, CA: Wadsworth Publishing, 1993); Steven A. Cohen, "Defining and Measuring Effectiveness in Public Management," *Public Productivity and Management Review* 17 (1993): 45–57; Mary Jo Bane, "Welfare Reform and Mandatory Versus Voluntary Work: Policy Issue or Management Problem?" *Journal of Policy Analysis and Management* 8 (1989): 285–89; Laurence E. Lynn Jr., *Managing Public Policy* (Boston: Little, Brown and Co., 1987); Laurence E. Lynn Jr., "The Reagan Administration and the Renitent Bureaucracy," in Lester M. Salamon and Michael S. Lund (eds.), *The Reagan Presidency and the Governing of America* (Washington, D.C.: Urban Institute, 1984): 339–70; Paul C. Light, "Does Management Matter?" *Governing Magazine* (Feb. 1, 1999); http://www.govexec.com/gpp/0299publicservice.htm. Date accessed: June 10, 2003.

3. See, for example, Hugh Heclo, *Government of Strangers* (Washington, D.C.: Brookings Institution, 1977); Herbert Kaufman, *Red Tape: Its Origins, Uses, and Abuses* (Washington, D.C.: Brookings Institution, 1977); Herbert Kaufman, *The Administrative Behavior of Federal Bureau Chiefs* (Washington, D.C.: Brookings Institution, 1981); David Nachmias and David H. Rosenbloom, *Bureaucratic Government, USA* (New York: St. Martin's Press, 1980).

4. See Michael Lipsky, *Street Level Bureaucrats: Dilemmas of the Individual in Public Services* (New York: Russell Sage, 1980); Michael Lipsky, "Bureaucratic Disentitlement in Social Welfare Programs," *Social Service Review* 58 (1984): 3–27; Jodi R. Sandfort, "Moving Beyond Discretion and Outcomes: Examining Public Management from the Front Lines of the Welfare System," *Journal of Public Administration Research and Theory* 10 (2000): 729–56; Steven Maynard-Moody and Michael C. Musheno, "State Agent or Citizen Agent: Two Narratives of Discretion," *Journal of Public Administration Research and Theory* 10 (2000): 329–58; Steven Maynard-Moody and Michael C. Musheno, *Cops, Teachers, Counselors: Stories from the Front Lines of Public Service* (Ann Arbor:

University of Michigan Press, 2003); Lael R. Keiser, "State Bureaucratic Discretion and the Administration of Social Welfare Programs: The Case of Social Security Disability," *Journal of Public Administration Research and Theory* 9 (1999): 87–107; Marcia K. Meyers, Bonnie Glaser, and Karin MacDonald, "On the Front Lines of Welfare Delivery: Are Workers Implementing Policy Reforms?" *Journal of Policy Analysis and Management* 17 (1998): 1–22; Marcia K. Meyers and Susan Vorsanger, "Street-Level Bureaucrats and the Implementation of Public Policy," in B. Guy Peters and Jon Pierre (eds.), *Handbook of Public Administration* (Thousand Oaks, CA: Sage Publications, 2003), 245–55; Patrick G. Scott, "Assessing Determinants of Bureaucratic Discretion: An Experiment in Street-Level Decision Making," *Journal of Public Administration Research and Theory* 7 (1997): 35–57; Marisa Kelly, "Theories of Justice and Street-Level Discretion," *Journal of Public Administration Research and Theory* 4 (1994): 119–40; Mary Jo Bane and David T. Ellwood, *Welfare Realities: From Rhetoric to Reform* (Cambridge, MA: Harvard University Press, 1994).

5. See Douglas Morgan et al., "What Middle Managers Do in Local Government. *Public Administration Review* 56:4 (1996): 359–66.

6. See D. H. Rosenbloom, *Public Administration: Understanding Management, Politics and Law in the Public Sector,* 4th edition (New York: McGraw-Hill, 1998).

7. Morgan, "What Middle Managers Do."

8. See, for example, Anne M. Khademian, "Is Silly Putty Manageable? Looking for the Links between Culture, Management, and Context," in Jeffrey L. Brudney, Laurence J. O'Toole Jr., and Hal G. Rainey (eds.), *Advancing Public Management* (Washington, D.C.: Georgetown University Press, 2000), 33–48, who points out that it is important to understand the "interdependencies between leadership and *context*" (34, emphasis added). See also Rainey, *Understanding and Managing Public Organizations.*

9. See Maynard-Moody and Musheno, *Cops, Teachers, Counselors.*

10. See Maynard-Moody and Musheno, *Cops, Teachers, Counselors*; Sandfort, "Moving Beyond Discretion"; Khademian, "Is Silly Putty Manageable?"; Kristen Dellinger, "Wearing Gender and Sexuality 'On Your Sleeve': Dress Norms and the Importance of Occupational and Organizational Culture at Work." *Gender Issues* 20 (2002): 3–25; Janet Coble Vinzant and Lane Crothers, *Street-Level Leadership: Discretion and Legitimacy in Front-Line Public Service* (Washington, D.C.: Georgetown University Press, 1998); Harrison M. Trice, *Occupational Subcultures in the Workplace* (Ithaca, NY: Industrial and Labor Relations Press, 1993); Edgar H. Schein, "What You Need to Know about Organizational Culture," *Training and Development Journal* 40 (1986): 30–33; Harrison M. Trice and Janice M. Beyer, *The Culture of Work Organizations* (Englewood Cliffs, NJ: Prentice Hall, 1992).

11. See, for example, Denhardt, *The Pursuit of Significance*; Behn, *Leadership Counts.*

12. See, for example, Meier and O'Toole, "Managerial Strategies"; Ingraham, Joyce, and Kneedler Donahue, *Government Performance*; Patricia W. Ingraham and Amy Kneedler Donahue, "Dissecting the Black Box Revisited: Characterizing Government Management Capacity," in Carolyn J. Heinrich and Laurence E. Lynn, Jr. (eds.), *Governance and Performance: New Perspectives* (Washington, D.C.: Georgetown University Press, 2000), 292–318; Sandfort, "Moving Beyond Discretion"; Lawrence M. Mead, "The Decline of Welfare in Wisconsin," *Journal of Public Administration Research and Theory* 9 (1999): 597–622; Saundra K. Schneider, William G. Jacoby, and Jerrell D. Coggburn, "The Structure of Bureaucratic Decisions in the American States," *Public Administration Review* 57 (1997): 240–49.

13. See, for example, James P. Guthrie, "High-Involvement Work Practices, Turnover, and Productivity: Evidence from New Zealand," *Academy of Management Journal* 44 (2001): 180–92; John A. Wagner III and Jeffrey A. LePine, "Effects of Participation on Performance and Satisfaction: Additional Meta-analytic Evidence," *Psychological Reports* 84 (1999): 719–26; Ingraham, Thompson, and Sanders, *Transforming Government*; Terry, *Leadership of Public Bureaucracies*; Riccucci, *Unsung Heroes.*

14. See, for example, Robert T. Nakamura and Frank Smallwood, *The Politics of Policy Implementation* (New York: St. Martin's Press, 1980), and Francis E. Rourke, *Bureaucracy, Politics and Public Policy*, 2d ed. (Boston: Little, Brown and Co., 1976).

15. See Lipsky, *Street Level Bureaucrats*; Lipsky, "Bureaucratic Disentitlement"; Maynard-Moody and Musheno, *Cops, Teachers, Counselors*; Maynard-Moody and Musheno, "State Agency"; Sandfort, "Moving Beyond Discretion"; Schneider, Jacoby, and Coggburn, "Structure of Bureaucratic Decisions."

16. Richard F. Elmore, "Backward Mapping: Implementation Research and Policy Decisions," *Political Science Quarterly* 94 (1979–80): 601–16.

17. See, for example, Lipsky, *Street Level Bureaucrats*; Maynard-Moody and Musheno, *Cops, Teachers, Counselors.*

18. See Yeheskel Hasenfeld (ed.), *Human Services as Complex Organizations* (Newbury Park, CA: Sage, 1992).

19. Sandfort, "Moving Beyond Discretion," 731.

20. Thomas L. Gais and Richard P. Nathan, *Status Report on the Occasion of the 5th Anniversary of the 1996 Personal Responsibility Welfare-Reform Act* (Albany, NY: Nelson A. Rockefeller Institute of Government, 2001).

21. This model is based on a model developed for the larger study on welfare reform conducted with funding from the U.S. Department of Health and

Human Services (HHS) and the Rockefeller Institute of Government in Albany, New York.

22. States were selected from a larger sample of twenty states included in the Rockefeller Institute of Government's "State Capacity Study" (Nathan and Gais, *Status Report*).

23. "Clients" are included in this study to the extent they are seeking to recertify for TANF benefits.

Chapter 2. Ending Welfare as We Knew It

1. It should be noted that Bane, one of the country's most prominent scholars and authorities on welfare issues, later resigned her post in protest over President Clinton's decision to sign the welfare bill.

2. See Eugene Bardach, *Improving the Productivity of JOBS Programs* (New York: MDRC, 1993).

3. See www.aphsa.org/Policy/HistoryWelfare.asp, American Public Human Services Association. Date accessed: June 1, 2003.

4. In the period between 1988 and 1996, a number of states used the federal "waiver" process, securing exemptions from certain aspects of the AFDC legislation, to develop employment-focused reform programs at the state level. Michigan, for example, conducted demonstrations of a "Project Zero" approach, which seeks to reduce to zero the number of families on assistance without earned income. Wisconsin adopted an even more radical experiment, in which welfare benefits were largely replaced by private or public sector employment.

5. See Thomas L. Gais and Richard P. Nathan, *Status Report on the Occasion of the 5th Anniversary of the 1996 Personal Responsibility Welfare-Reform Act* (Albany, NY: The Nelson A. Rockefeller Institute of Government, August, 2001); Yeheskel Hasenfeld, "Social Services and Welfare-to-Work: Prospects for the Social Work Profession," *Administration in Social Work* 23 (2000): 185–99; Yeheskel Hasenfeld, "Organizational Forms as Moral Practices: The Case of Welfare Departments," *Social Service Review* 74 (2000): 329–51; Lawrence M. Mead, "The Decline of Welfare in Wisconsin," *Journal of Public Administration Research and Theory* 9 (1999): 597–622; Marcia K. Meyers, Bonnie Glaser, and Karin MacDonald, "On the Front Lines of Welfare Delivery: Are Workers Implementing Policy Reforms?" *Journal of Policy Analysis and Management* 17 (1998): 1–22.

6. U.S. General Accounting Office (GAO), *States Are Restructuring Programs to Reduce Welfare Dependence* (Washington, D.C.: U.S. GAO, 1998).

7. U.S. Health and Human Services (HHS), *Temporary Assistance for Needy Families (TANF) Program* (Washington, D.C.: U.S. HHS, 1998).

8. *State Capacity Report, Texas* (Albany, NY: The Nelson A. Rockefeller Institute of Government, 1998).

9. Many DHS workers moved to the Texas Workforce Commission. And Lockheed Martin hired sixty-six TWC employees/former DHS workers.

10. *State Capacity Report, Texas.*

11. Ibid.

12. Ann-Marie Imbornoni, "George Walker Bush: A Son of a President, Now President." January 15, 2001. http://www.factmonster.com/index.html. Date accessed: June 1, 2003.

13. The Division of Family and Children Services (DFCS) is nested in the state's Department of Human Resources.

14. *State Capacity Report, Georgia* (Albany, NY: The Nelson A. Rockefeller Institute of Government, 1998).

15. See www2.state.ga.us/Departments/DHR/tanf.html, State of Georgia. Date accessed: June 4, 2003.

16. *State Capacity Report, Georgia.*

17. See www.naco.org/programs/social/welfare/W_reform/MNIMBE .htm, National Association of Counties. Date accessed: June 4, 2003.

18. Waivers permit states to circumvent federal law in order to experiment with changes or reforms to welfare in their states.

19. *State Capacity Report, Michigan* (Albany, NY: The Nelson A. Rockefeller Institute of Government, 1998), 12.

20. *State Capacity Report, Michigan.*

21. The Michigan House of Representatives held three public hearings in three days, and the public testified at only two of these hearings.

22. The bill was ultimately passed with a twelve-month exemption from Michigan's Administrative Procedure Act. This exemption was lifted in 1997.

23. *State Capacity Report, Michigan,* 9.

24. *State Capacity Report, Michigan.*

25. The Michigan Jobs Commission was initially created via executive order as a limited-term (two years) agency in February of 1993 and became a department in February of 1995. For the most part, it was a consolidation of government programs, especially in workforce development. The economic development function was moved from the Commerce Department (which later became a regulatory agency and was renamed). Approximately fifty job training programs were consolidated from ten different state departments into the Jobs Commission.

26. *State Capacity Report, New York* (Albany, NY: The Nelson A. Rockefeller Institute of Government, 1998).

27. Hasenfeld, "Social Services and Welfare-to-Work," 189.

Chapter 3. The Important Role of Public Management in Welfare Reform

1. See, for example, H. George Frederickson and Kevin B. Smith, *The Public Administration Theory Primer* (Boulder, CO: Westview Press, 2003); Kenneth J. Meier and Laurence J. O'Toole Jr., "Managerial Strategies and Behavior in Networks: A Model with Evidence from U.S. Public Education," *Journal of Public Administration Research and Theory* 11 (2001): 271–93; Kenneth J. Meier and Laurence J. O'Toole Jr., "Public Management and Organizational Performance: The Effect of Managerial Quality," *Journal of Public Administration Research and Theory* 12 (2002): 629–43; Hal G. Rainey and Paula Steinbauer, "Galloping Elephants: Developing Elements of a Theory of Effective Government Organizations," *Journal of Public Administration Research and Theory* 9 (1999): 1–32; Robert D. Behn, "What Right Do Public Managers Have to Lead?" *Public Administration Review* (1998). 209–25; Robert D. Behn, "Creating an Innovative Organization: Ten Hints for Involving Frontline Workers," *State and Local Government Review* 27 (1995): 221–34; Robert D. Behn, *Leadership Counts* (Cambridge: Harvard University Press, 1991); Hal G. Rainey, *Understanding and Managing Public Organizations* (San Francisco: Jossey-Bass, 1997). Norma M. Riccucci, *Unsung Heroes: Federal Execucrats Making a Difference* (Washington, D.C.: Georgetown University Press, 1996); Larry D. Terry, *Leadership of Public Bureaucracies: The Administrator as Conservator* (Thousand Oaks, CA: Sage Publications, 1995); Robert B. Denhardt, *The Pursuit of Significance: Strategies for Managerial Success in Public Organizations* (Belmont, CA: Wadsworth Publishing, 1993); Eugene Bardach, *Improving the Productivity of JOBS Programs* (New York: MDRC, 1993); Laurence E. Lynn Jr., *Managing Public Policy* (Boston: Little, Brown and Co., 1987); Laurence E. Lynn Jr., "The Reagan Administration and the Renitent Bureaucracy," in Lester M. Salamon and Michael S. Lund (eds.), *The Reagan Presidency and the Governing of America* (Washington, D.C.: Urban Institute, 1984), 339–70; Paul C. Light, "Does Management Matter?" *Governing Magazine* (Feb. 1, 1999), http://www.govexec.com/gpp/0299publicservice.htm. Date accessed: June 10, 2003.

2. See, for example, Patricia W. Ingraham, Philip G. Joyce, and Amy Kneedler Donahue, *Government Performance: Why Management Matters* (Baltimore: Johns Hopkins University Press, 2003); Jerrell D. Coggburn and Saundra K. Schneider, "The Quality of Management and Government Performance: An Empirical Analysis of the American States," *Public Administration Review* 63 (2003): 206–13; Carolyn J. Heinrich and Laurence E. Lynn Jr., "Government and Performance: The Influence of Programs Structure and Management on Job Training Partnership Act (JTPA) Program Outcomes,"

in Carolyn Heinrich and Laurence E. Lynn Jr. (eds.), *Governance and Performance: New Perspectives* (Washington, D.C.: Georgetown University Press, 2000); Jodi R. Sandfort, "Moving beyond Discretion and Outcomes: Examining Public Management from the Front Lines of the Welfare System," *Journal of Public Administration Research and Theory* 10 (2000): 729–56; Laurence J. O'Toole Jr. and Kenneth J. Meier, "Networks, Hierarchies, and Public Management: Modeling and Nonlinearities," in Carolyn Heinrich and Laurence E. Lynn Jr. (eds.), *Governance and Performance: New Perspectives* (Washington, D.C.: Georgetown University Press, 2000); Lawrence M. Mead, "The Decline of Welfare in Wisconsin," *Journal of Public Administration Research and Theory* 9 (1999): 597–622; Edward T. Jennings Jr. and Jo Ann G. Ewalt, "Interorganizational Coordination, Administrative Consolidation, and Policy Performance," *Public Administration Review* 58 (1998): 417–28; H. Brinton Milward and Keith G. Provan, "Principles for Controlling Agents: The Political Economy of Network Structures," *Journal of Public Administration Research and Theory* 8 (1998): 203–22.

3. Patricia W. Ingraham and Amy Kneedler Donahue, "Dissecting the Black Box Revisited: Characterizing Government Management Capacity," in Carolyn J. Heinrich and Laurence E. Lynn Jr. (eds.), *Governance and Performance: New Perspectives* (Washington, D.C.: Georgetown University Press, 2000), 292–318, at p. 294.

4. Ibid.

5. Coggburn and Schneider, "The Quality of Management."

6. See, for example, Patricia W. Ingraham, James R. Thompson, and Ronald P. Sanders, *Transforming Government* (San Francisco: Jossey-Bass, 1998); Mark Moore, *Creating Public Value* (Cambridge, MA: Harvard University Press, 1997); Terry, *Leadership of Public Bureaucracies*; Riccucci, *Unsung Heroes*; Steven A. Cohen, "Defining and Measuring Effectiveness in Public Management," *Public Productivity and Management Review* 17 (1993): 45–57; Steven A. Cohen and William Eimicke, *The New Effective Public Manager* (San Francisco: Jossey-Bass, 1995); Denhardt, *The Pursuit of Significance*; Behn, *Leadership Counts*.

7. Denhardt, *The Pursuit of Significance*. See also Robert B. Denhardt and Janet Vinzant Denhardt, *Leadership for Change: Case Studies in American Local Government* (Arlington, VA: PricewaterhouseCoopers Endowment for the Business of Government, 1999); Janet Vinzant Denhardt and Robert B. Denhardt, *Creating a Culture of Innovation: 10 Lessons from America's Best Run City* (Arlington, VA: PricewaterhouseCoopers Endowment for the Business of Government, 2001).

8. Meier and O'Toole, "Managerial Strategies."

9. See, for example, Steven Hutchison, Kathleen E. Valentino, and Sandra L. Kirkner, "What Works for the Gander Does Not Work as Well for the Goose: The Effects of Leader Behavior," *Journal of Applied Social Psychology* 28 (1998):

171–83; Casey Ichniowski, Kathryn Shaw, and Giovanna Prennushi, "The Effects of Human Resource Management Practices on Productivity: A Study of Steel Finishing Lines," *American Economic Review* 87 (1997): 291–314; Judith L. Komaki, "Toward Effective Supervision: An Operant Analysis and Comparison of Managers at Work," *Journal of Applied Psychology* 71 (1986): 270–80.

10. See, for example, James P. Guthrie, "High-Involvement Work Practices, Turnover, and Productivity: Evidence from New Zealand," *Academy of Management Journal* 44 (2001): 180–92; Institute of Industrial Engineers (IIE), "Cynical Employees Created by Bad Management," *Solutions Magazine* 32 (2000): 74; John A. Wagner III and Jeffrey A. LePine, "Effects of Participation on Performance and Satisfaction: Additional Meta-analytic Evidence," *Psychological Reports* 84 (1999): 719–26; Ichniowski, Shaw, and Prennushi, "The Effects of Human Resource."

11. Hutchison, Valentino, and Kirkner, "What Works for the Gander."

12. David Osbourne and Tom Gaebler, *Reinventing Government* (Reading, MA: Addison-Wesley, 1992); John M. Kamensky, "The Role of 'Re-inventing Government' in Federal Management Reform," *Public Administration Review* 56 (1996): 247–55.

13. Laurence E. Lynn Jr., "The Myth of the Bureaucratic Paradigm: What Traditional Public Administration Stood For," *Public Administration Review* 61 (2001): 144–60; Charles Goodsell, "Reinventing Government or Rediscovering It?" *Public Administration Review* 53 (1993): 85–86; James D. Carroll, "The Rhetoric of Reform and Political Reality in the National Performance Review," *Public Administration Review* 55 (1995): 302–12; Ronald C. Moe, "The 'Reinventing Government' Exercise: Misinterpreting the Problem, Misjudging the Consequences," *Public Administration Review* 54 (1994): 111–22.

14. See, for example, Mead, "The Decline of Welfare"; Behn, *Leadership Counts*; Edward T. Jennings Jr., and Jo Ann G. Ewalt, "Interorganizational Coordination, Administrative Consolidation, and Policy Performance," *Public Administration Review* 58 (1998): 417–28; Wendy P. Crook, "Trickle-Down Bureaucracy: Does the Organization Affect Client Responses to Programs?" *Administration in Social Work* 26 (2001): 37–59; P. S. Ramsdell, empirical study. "Staff Participation in Organizational Decision-Making: An Empirical Study," *Administration in Social Work* 18 (1994): 51–71; S. Malka, "Managerial Behavior, Participation, and Effectiveness in Social Welfare Organizations," *Administration in Social Work* 13 (1989): 47–65; R. A. Weatherley, "Participating Management in Public Welfare: What Are the Prospects?" *Administration in Social Work* 7 (1983): 39–49.

15. Behn, *Leadership Counts*, 216–17.

16. Mead, "The Decline of Welfare," 609.

17. In Michigan, however, one aspect of job services—child care—remains in the welfare office.

18. As of this writing, 39 states require that single adult recipients receiving TANF participate in work activities for a set number of hours per week, whereas ten determine hours of participation on an individual basis; two states allow localities to set the required hours of participation. In fiscal year 2000, the majority of states with a fixed hourly participation requirement set the number of hours at the federal participation rate level of 30 hours per week (27 of the 39 states). Some, however, set it lower: Missouri, North Dakota, and South Dakota allow adult recipients with children under age 6 to work only 20 hours per week, whereas requirements in Connecticut, Idaho, Louisiana, New Mexico, and Rhode Island range from 20 to 29 hours per week. Other states set higher work expectations: Alabama, Arizona, California, Hawaii, Tennessee, and Vermont have requirements ranging from 32 to 40 hours per week. Tennessee, however, allows adult recipients with low basic skills to work only 20 hours per week, and Vermont does the same for adult recipients with children under age 13. Of course, workers can use their discretion to exempt persons from the work requirement. See www.cnponline.org/index.html, Center for National Policy. Date accessed: July 10, 2003.

19. Sandfort, "Moving beyond Discretion"; James Q. Wilson, *Bureaucracy: What Government Agencies Do and Why They Do It* (New York: Basic Books, 1989).

20. Yeheskel Hasenfeld, who illustrates how clients' needs are sometimes overshadowed during the in-take or assessment process. "Social Services and Welfare-to-Work: Prospects for the Social Work Profession," *Administration in Social Work* 23 (2000): 185–99.

21. Wallace Sayre, "The Triumph of Techniques over Purpose," *Public Administration Review* 8 (1948): 134–37.

22. Of course, deterrence may be an implicit goal in the other sites. Not surprisingly, though, managers and officials may not be willing to explicitly disclose this goal.

23. In New York, however, the most important goal to workers was "treating clients fairly and equitably."

24. See, for example, Hasenfeld, "Social Services and Welfare-to-Work."

25. See Edgar H. Schein, "What You Need to Know about Organizational Culture," *Training and Development Journal* 40 (1986): 30–33.

26. For an excellent treatment of the complexity and overlapping nature of bureaucratic goals and objectives, see David Nachmias and David H. Rosenbloom, *Bureaucratic Government, USA* (New York: St. Martin's Press, 1980).

27. See, Laurence E. Lynn Jr., *Public Management as Art, Science, and Profession* (Chatham, NJ: Chatham House Publishers, 1996).

Chapter 4. Public Management and Street-Level Bureaucrats

1. See Beryl A. Radin, *Beyond Machiavelli: Policy Analysis Comes of Age* (Washington, D.C.: Georgetown University Press, 2000); Beryl A. Radin, *The Accountable Juggler: The Art of Leadership in a Federal Agency* (Washington, D.C.: Congressional Quarterly Press, 2002); D. H. Rosenbloom, *Public Administration: Understanding Management, Politics and Law in the Public Sector,* 4th ed. (McGraw-Hill: New York, 1998); L. E. Lynn Jr., *Managing Public Policy* (Boston: Little, Brown and Co., 1987); Robert T. Nakamura and Frank Smallwood, *The Politics of Policy Implementation* (New York: St. Martin's Press, 1980).

2. Richard F. Elmore, "Backward Mapping: Implementation Research and Policy Decisions," *Political Science Quarterly* 94 (1979–80): 601–16.

3. See also Arthur M. Recesso, "First Year Implementation of the School to Work Opportunities Act Policy: An Effort at Backward Mapping," *Education Policy Analysis Archives,* 7:11 (1999).

4. See, for example, Michael Lipsky, *Street Level Bureaucrats: Dilemmas of the Individual in Public Services* (New York: Russell Sage, 1980); Michael Lipsky, "Bureaucratic Disentitlement in Social Welfare Programs," *Social Service Review* 58 (1984): 3–27; Marisa Kelly, "Theories of Justice and Street-Level Discretion," *Journal of Public Administration Research and Theory* 4 (1994): 119–40; Carol S. Weissert, "Beyond the Organization: The Influence of Community and Personal Values on Street-Level Bureaucrats' Responsiveness," *Journal of Public Administration Research and Theory* 4 (1994): 225–55; Saundra K. Schneider and William G. Jacoby, "Influences on Bureaucratic Policy Initiatives in the American States," *Journal of Public Administration Research and Theory* 6 (1996): 495–522; Saundra K. Schneider, William G. Jacoby, and Jerrell D. Coggburn, "The Structure of Bureaucratic Decisions in the American States," *Public Administration Review* 57 (1997): 240–49; Patrick G. Scott, "Assessing Determinants of Bureaucratic Discretion: An Experiment in Street-Level Decision Making," *Journal of Public Administration Research and Theory* 7 (1997): 35–57; Marcia K. Meyers, Bonnie Glaser, and Karin MacDonald, "On the Front Lines of Welfare Delivery: Are Workers Implementing Policy Reforms?" *Journal of Policy Analysis and Management* 17 (1998): 1–22; Lael R. Keiser, "State Bureaucratic Discretion and the Administration of Social Welfare Programs: The Case of Social Security Disability," *Journal of Public Administration Research and Theory* 9 (1999): 87–107; Jodi R. Sandfort, "Moving beyond Discretion and Outcomes: Examining Public Management from the Front Lines of the Welfare System," *Journal of Public Administration Research and Theory* 10 (2000): 729–56; Steven Maynard-Moody and Michael C. Musheno, *Cops, Teachers, Counselors: Stories from the Front Lines of Public Service* (Ann Arbor: University

of Michigan Press, 2003); Steven Maynard-Moody and Michael C. Musheno, "State Agency or Citizen Agent: Two Narratives of Discretion," *Journal of Public Administration Research and Theory* 10 (2000): 329–58.

5. Lipsky, *Street Level Bureaucrats*, 13.

6. Maynard-Moody and Musheno, "State Agency," 334.

7. Maynard-Moody and Musheno, *Cops, Teachers, Counselors*, 10. See also H. George Frederickson, *The Spirit of Public Administration* (San Francisco: Jossey-Bass, 1997).

8. See, for example, Janet Coble Vinzant and Lane Crothers, *Street-Level Leadership: Discretion and Legitimacy in Front-Line Public Service* (Washington, D.C.: Georgetown University Press, 1998).

9. Yeheskel Hasenfeld (ed.), *Human Services as Complex Organizations* (Newbury Park, CA: Sage, 1992).

10. Scott, "Assessing Determinants," 37.

11. Keiser, "State Bureaucratic Discretion." See also, for example, J.F. Handler, *The Conditions of Discretion: Autonomy, Community, Bureaucracy* (New York: Russell Sage, 1986); Weissert, "Beyond the Organization."

12. Keiser, "State Bureaucratic Discretion," 88.

13. See Keiser, "State Bureaucratic Discretion" and Carolyn L. Clark-Daniels and R. Steven Daniels, "Street-Level Decision Making in Elder Mistreatment Policy: An Empirical Case Study of Service Rationing," *Social Science Quarterly* 76 (1995): 460–73. Also, Marcia K. Meyers and Susan Vorsanger, who point to research showing that political officials have little control over street-level bureaucratic behavior in, "Street-Level Bureaucrats and the Implementation of Public Policy," in B. Guy Peters and Jon Pierre (eds.), *Handbook of Public Administration* (Thousand Oaks, CA: Sage Publications, 2003), 245–55.

14. See, for example, T. Pesso, "Local Welfare Offices: Managing the Intake Process," *Public Policy* 26 (1978): 305–30; Jeffrey Manditch Prottas, *People-Processing: The Street-Level Bureaucrat in Public Service Bureaucracies* (Lexington, MA: Lexington Books, 1979); Kelly, "Theories of Justice"; Scott, "Assessing Determinants"; Keiser, "State Bureaucratic Discretion"; Sandfort, "Moving Beyond Discretion."

15. Scott, "Assessing Determinants."

16. See, for example, Maynard-Moody and Musheno, "State Agency"; Maynard-Moody and Musheno, *Cops, Teachers, Counselors*; C. N. Stone, "Attitudinal Tendencies among Officials," in Charles Goodsell (ed.), *The Public Encounter: Where State and Citizen Meet* (Bloomington: Indiana University Press, 1981); Charles Goodsell, "Client Evaluation of Three Welfare Programs," *Administration and Society* 12 (1980): 123–36; Charles Goodsell, "Looking Once Again at Human Service Bureaucracy," *Journal of Politics* 43 (1981): 763–78;

R. Paviour, "The Influence of Class and Race on Clinical Assessments by MSW Students," *Social Service Review* 62 (1988): 684–93; Kelly, "Theories of Justice"; Weissert, "Beyond the Organization"; Meyers, Glaser, and MacDonald, "On the Front Lines"; Marcia K. Meyers and Nara Dillon, "Institutional Paradoxes: Why Welfare Workers Can't Reform Welfare," in H. George Frederickson and Jocelyn M. Johnston (eds.), *Public Administration Reform and Innovation* (Tuscaloosa: University of Alabama Press, 1999): 230–58; Meyers and Vorsanger, "Street-Level Bureaucrats"; Jodi Sandfort, "The Structural Impediments of Human Service Collaboration: The Case of Front-Line Welfare Reform Implementation," *Social Service Review* 73 (1999): 314–39; Ann Chih Lin, *Reform in the Making: The Implementation of Social Policy in Prison* (Princeton, NJ: Princeton University Press, 2000). In "State Bureaucratic Discretion," Keiser examines the effects of broader, macro-level factors such as the political environment and the economic environment on bureaucratic discretion, as measured by the percentage of people who receive disability benefits in each of the fifty states.

17. Sandfort, "Moving beyond Discretion." It is important to note that she *infers* that traditional public administrative practices characterize public welfare agencies (i.e., those responsible for income maintenance functions) and that the new public management characterizes the private welfare-to-work programs (i.e., those responsible for delivering the employment programs to welfare clients).

18. Mary Parker Follett, *Creative Experience* (New York: Longmans, Green Publishers, 1924); Mary Parker Follett, *The New State: Group Organization, the Solution of Popular Government* (New York: Longmans, Green Publishers, 1918); Chester Barnard, *The Functions of the Executive* (Cambridge, MA: Harvard University Press, 1938).

19. Sandfort, "Moving beyond Discretion," 751.

20. Scott, "Assessing Determinants." See also Maynard-Moody and Musheno, *Cops, Teachers, Counselors.*

21. Principal component analysis was utilized for identifying the three underlying goal dimensions. Based on this analysis, the three summative goal indices (standardized by the number of included questions) were constructed. It should be noted that a good deal of information on the clerical activities associated with eligibility determination was not captured by the hand recording of encounters (i.e., in New York and Georgia, tape recording of encounters was not allowed). For example, a typical application for assistance requires the case workers to ask a series of questions to determine whether certain basic eligibility rules for TANF can be met. Such questions would include amount of earnings, whether child support is received, whether there are contribu-

tions from household or family members, and amount of monthly expenditures. Because this information was not captured and ultimately coded, the data on amount of time devoted to eligibility determination may be incomplete. See also Norma M. Riccucci, Marcia K. Meyers, Irene Lurie, and Jun Seop Han, "The Implementation of Welfare Reform Policy: The Role of Public Managers in Front-Line Practices," *Public Administration Review* 64 (2004): 438–48.

22. Lipsky, *Street Level Bureaucrats.*

23. Meyers and Vorsanger, "Street-Level Bureaucrats."

24. A dummy variable was created where 0 = "state-administered" (for Michigan and Texas) and 1 = "county-administered" or "both county- and state-administered" (for New York and Georgia).

25. Scott, "Assessing Determinants."

26. Sandfort, "Moving beyond Discretion."

27. John Brehm and Scott Gates, *Working, Shirking and Sabotage: Bureaucratic Response to a Democratic Public* (Ann Arbor: University of Michigan Press, 1997).

28. Meyers and Vorsanger, "Street-Level Bureaucrats," 248. See also Maynard-Moody and Musheno, *Cops, Teachers, Counselors*; Kirsten Dellinger, "Wearing Gender and Sexuality 'On Your Sleeve': Dress Norms and the Importance of Occupational and Organizational Culture at Work," *Gender Issues* 20 (2002): 3–25; Anne M. Khademian, "Is Silly Putty Manageable? Looking for the Links between Culture, Management, and Context," in Jeffrey L. Brudney, Laurence J. O'Toole Jr., and Hal G. Rainey (eds.), *Advancing Public Management* (Washington, D.C.: Georgetown University Press, 2000), 33–48; Hal G. Rainey, *Understanding and Managing Public Organizations* (San Francisco: Jossey-Bass, 1997); Harrison M. Trice, *Occupational Subcultures in the Workplace* (Ithaca, NY: Industrial and Labor Relations Press, 1993); Edgar H. Schein, *Organizational Culture and Leadership*, 2d edition (San Francisco: Jossey-Bass, 1992); Abraham Sagie and Jacob Weisberg, "A Structural Analysis of Behavior in Work Situations shared by Group Members," *Journal of Psychology* 130 (1996): 371–81.

29. Lipsky, *Street Level Bureaucrats*, 27.

30. Sandfort, "Moving beyond Discretion."

31. See, for example, Kenneth J. Meier and John Bohte, "Structure and Discretion: Missing Links in Representative Bureaucracy," *Journal of Public Administration Research and Theory* 11 (2001): 455–70; Kenneth J. Meier, "Latinos and Representative Bureaucracy: Testing the Thompson and Henderson Hypotheses," *Journal of Public Administration Research and Theory* 3 (1993): 393–415; Lael R. Keiser, Vicky M. Wilkins, Kenneth J. Meier, and Catherine Holland, "Lipstick and Logarithms: Gender, Institutional Context, and Representative Bureaucracy," *American Political Science Review* 96 (2002): 553–64; Norma M.

Riccucci and Judith R. Saidel, "The Representativeness of State-Level Bureaucratic Leaders: A Missing Piece of the Representative Bureaucracy Puzzle," *Public Administration Review* 57 (1997): 423–30.

32. However, it is important to note that only 1 to 14 percent of the variation in street-level behavior can be explained by these models.

33. Of course, one could also argue that over time, workers, especially in the social services, become immune to their clients, treating them more as cases rather than people. See Scott, "Assessing Determinants."

34. Sandfort, "Moving beyond Discretion." See also Elton Mayo's classic Hawthorne studies, as described by Fritz J. Rothlisberger and William J. Dickson, *Management and the Worker: An Account of Research Conducted by the Western Electric Company, Hawthorne Works, Chicago* (Cambridge, MA: Harvard University Press, 1967).

35. See Trice, *Occupational Subcultures*.

36. Maynard-Moody and Musheno, *Cops, Teachers, Counselors*, 4.

37. Jocelyn J. Johnston and Cherita L. McIntye find a link between organization culture and job satisfaction in, "Organizational Culture and Climate Correlates of Job Satisfaction," *Psychological Reports* 82 (1998): 851–60.

38. See, for example, Edward E. Lawler III, and Lyman W. Porter, "The Effect of Performance on Job Satisfaction," *Industrial Relations* 7 (1967): 20–28, in which the authors argued that performance causes job satisfaction rather than the other way around. Lyman W. Porter and Edward E. Lawler III, *Managerial Attitudes and Performance* (Homewood, IL: Richard D. Irwin, 1968) also advanced the expectancy theory of motivation, which states that people are motivated based on their perception of how likely their work is to lead to successful performance. Compare the classic work of Frederick Herzberg, *Work and the Nature of Man* (New York: Mentor Executive Library, 1966).

39. See, for example, Johnston and McIntyre, "Organizational Culture"; Ronald J. Burke, "Management Practices, Employees' Satisfaction and Perceptions of Quality Service," *Psychological Reports* 77 (1995): 748–50; James L. Heskett, W. Earl Sasser, and Christopher W. L. Hart, *Service Breakthroughs* (New York: Free Press, 1990).

40. Kenneth N. Wexley and Gary A. Yukl, *Organization Behavior and Personnel Psychology*, rev. ed. (Homewood, IL: Richard D. Irwin, Inc., 1984), 65, 66.

41. See, for example, Hugh Heclo, *Government of Strangers* (Washington, D.C.: Brookings Institution, 1977); Herbert Kaufman, *Red Tape: Its Origins, Uses, and Abuses* (Washington, D.C.: Brookings Institution, 1977); Herbert Kaufman, *The Administrative Behavior of Federal Bureau Chiefs* (Washington, D.C.: Brookings Institution, 1981); David Nachmias and David H. Rosenbloom, *Bureaucratic Government, USA* (New York: St. Martin's Press, 1980);

Mary Jo Bane and David T. Ellwood, *Welfare Realities: From Rhetoric to Reform* (Cambridge, MA: Harvard University Press, 1994).

Chapter 5. The Art and Science of Managing Street-Level Bureaucrats

1. Jodi R. Sandfort, "Moving beyond Discretion and Outcomes: Examining Public Management from the Front Lines of the Welfare System," *Journal of Public Administration Research and Theory* 10 (2000): 729–56, 751.

2. Frederick C. Mosher, *Democracy and the Public Service* (New York: Oxford University Press, 1968). See also Dwight Waldo, *The Enterprise of Public Administration* (Novato, CA: Chandler and Sharp Publishers, Inc., 1980).

3. Mosher, *Democracy.*

4. Ibid., 111.

5. See also Sandfort, "Moving beyond Discretion."

6. Steven Maynard-Moody and Michael C. Musheno, *Cops, Teachers, Counselors: Stories from the Front Lines of Public Service* (Ann Arbor: University of Michigan Press, 2003), 8.

7. Sandfort, "Moving beyond Discretion," 751.

8. The same information about the shortcomings associated with the hand recording of encounters discussed in chapter 4, note 21, applies here.

9. See the online report on privatizing under welfare reform, http://aspe .hhs.gov/hsp/privatization-rpt03/privreport.htm#II, Assistant Secretary for Planning and Evaluation, U.S. Department of Health and Human Services. Date accessed: August 10, 2003.

10. See, for example, Irene Lurie and Norma M. Riccucci, "Changing the 'Culture' of Welfare Offices: From Vision to the Front Lines," *Administration and Society* 34 (2003): 653–77; R. H. Kilman, M. J. Saxton, and R. Serpa, "Issues in Understanding and Changing Culture," *California Management Review* 28 (1986): 87–94.

11. Edgar H. Schein, *Organizational Culture and Leadership,* 2d edition (San Francisco: Jossey-Bass, 1992), 12.

12. David Osborne and Ted Gaebler, *Reinventing Government: How the Entrepreneurial Spirit Is Transforming the Public Sector* (New York: Plume, 1993).

13. Anne M. Khademian, "Is Silly Putty Manageable? Looking for the links between Culture, Management, and Context," in Jeffrey L. Brudney, Laurence J. O'Toole Jr., and Hal G. Rainey (eds.), *Advancing Public Management* (Washington, D.C.: Georgetown University Press, 2000), 33–48, quotations 33–34, emphasis added.

14. See Harrison M. Trice, *Occupational Subcultures in the Workplace* (Ithaca, NY: Industrial and Labor Relations Press, 1993).

15. Khademian, "Is Silly Putty Manageable?" 35, emphasis added.

16. Thomas J. Kane and Mary Jo Bane, *Welfare Realities: From Rhetoric to Reform* (Cambridge, MA: Harvard University Press, 1994), 2, emphasis added.

17. See, Thomas L. Gais, "Welfare Reform: Findings in Brief" (Albany, NY: The Nelson A. Rockefeller Institute of Government, March 2002); Richard P. Nathan and Thomas L. Gais, *Implementing The Personal Responsibility Act of 1996: A First Look* (Albany, NY: The Nelson A. Rockefeller Institute of Government, 1999).

18. See, for example, Thomas J. Wang, Elizabeth Mort, Paul Nordberg, Yu-chiao Chang, Mary Cadigan, Laura Mylott, Lillian Ananian, B. Taylor Thompson, Michael Fessler, William Warren, Amy Wheeler, Mark Jordan, and Michael Fifer, "A Utilization Management Intervention to Reduce Unnecessary Testing in the Coronary Care Unit," *Archives of Internal Medicine* 162 (2002): 1885–90; Daniel H. Solomon, Hideki Hashimoto, Lawren Daltroy, and Matthew H. Liang, "Techniques to Improve Physicians' Use of Diagnostic Tests: A New Conceptual Framework," *Journal of the American Medical Association* 280 (1998): 2020–27; George D. Lundberg, "Changing Physician Behavior in Ordering Diagnostic Tests," *Journal of the American Medical Association* 280 (1998): 2036; Elizabeth Eckstrom and David M. Buchner, "Changing Physician Practice of Physical Activity Counseling," *Journal of General Internal Medicine* 14 (1999): 376–78; H. E. Nystrom, "Teaching and Learning in an Era of Change," Frontiers in Education Conference, 27th annual conference, November 5–8, 1997, *Proceedings,* vol. 2, 812–14; P. J. Greco and J. M. Eisenberg, "Changing Physicians' Practices," *New England Journal of Medicine* 329 (1993): 1271–74; W. H. Shaw and T. R. Manley, "Managing in a Global Environment," Institute of Electrical and Electronics Engineers (IEEE), Engineering Management Conference, October 25–28, 1992: 106–10; L. Allen, "The Engineered Communication," professional communication conference, October 30–November 1, 1991, *Proceedings,* vol. 2, 351–55; D. L. Hall and A. Nauda, "Management through the Year 2000: Gaining the Competitive Advantage," Institute of Electrical and Electronics Engineers (IEEE), Engineering Management Conference, October 21–24, 1990, 153–58.

19. See, for example, Wang et al., "A Utilization Management"; Eckstrom and Buchner, "Changing Physician Practice"; Lundberg, "Changing Physician Behavior"; Greco and Eisenberg, "Changing Physicians' Practices."

20. Daniel H. Solomon, Hideki Hashimoto, Lawren Daltroy, and Matthew H. Liang, "Techniques to Improve Physicians' Use of Diagnostic Tests: A New Conceptual Framework," *Journal of the American Medical Association* 280 (1998): 2020–27.

21. Laurence E. Lynn Jr., *Public Management as Art, Science, and Profession* (Chatham, NJ: Chatham House Publishers, 1996) 136.

22. Edgar H. Schein, "What You Need to Know about Organizational Culture," *Training and Development Journal* 40 (1986): 30–33.

23. See, for example, Wang et al., "A Utilization Management"; Lundberg, "Changing Physician Behavior"; Greco and Eisenberg, "Changing Physicians' Practices."

24. Greco and Eisenberg, "Changing Physicians' Practices," 1273.

25. Nystrom, "Teaching and Learning"; Greco and Eisenberg, "Changing Physicians' Practices"; Shaw and Manley, "Managing in a Global Environment."

26. Eckstrom and Buchner, "Changing Physician Practice"; Lundberg, "Changing Physician Behavior"; Nystrom, "Teaching and Learning"; Lynn, *Public Management*; Greco and Eisenberg, "Changing Physicians' Practices"; Shaw and Manley, "Managing in a Global Environment."

27. Solomon et al., "Techniques to Improve."

28. Greco and Eisenberg, "Changing Physicians' Practices," 1273.

Chapter 6. What Are Welfare Workers Doing at the Front Lines?

1. Sheila R. Zedlewski and Jennifer Holland studied data from a national survey administered in 2002 and found that only 37 percent of welfare recipients have information about when their welfare benefits will end. They also found that three out of four Spanish-speaking recipients are not aware of when their welfare benefits will end. *How Much Do Welfare Recipients Know about Time Limits?* (Washington, D.C.: Urban Institute, December 2003).

2. Or, if the applicant is a male, whether the spouse of the applicant is pregnant.

3. Based on this statistical analysis, it is uncertain to what degree workers actually responded to the clients' requests.

4. For a discussion of Max Weber's treatment of clients of government services, see David H. Rosenbloom, Robert S. Kravchuk, and Deborah Goldman Rosenbloom, *Public Administration: Understanding Management, Politics, and Law in the Public Sector*, 5th edition (New York: McGraw-Hill, 2002).

5. Steven Maynard-Moody and Michael C. Musheno, *Cops, Teachers, Counselors: Stories from the Front Lines of Public Service* (Ann Arbor: University of Michigan Press, 2003), 153–54.

6. See Evelyn Z. Brodkin, "Requiem for Welfare," *Dissent* 50 (2003): 29–36; Lawrence M. Mead, "Welfare Caseload Change: An Alternative Approach," *Policy Studies Journal* 31 (2003): 163–85; Lawrence M. Mead, "Caseload Change:

An Exploratory Study," *Journal of Policy Analysis and Management* 19 (2000): 465–72; LaDonna A. Pavetti, "Welfare Policy in Transition: Redefining the Social Contract for Poor Citizen Families with Children and for Immigrants," in S. H. Danziger and R. H. Haveman (eds.), *Understanding Poverty* (New York: Russell Sage Foundation, 2001), 229–77; Thomas L. Gais and Richard P. Nathan, *Status Report on the Occasion of the 5th Anniversary of the 1996 Personal Responsibility Welfare-Reform Act* (Albany, NY: The Nelson A. Rockefeller Institute of Government, August 2001); Alvin L. Schorr, *Welfare Reform: Failure and Remedies* (Westport, CT: Praeger Publishers, 2001).

7. See, for example, Kristine Siefert and Srinika Jayaratne, "Job Satisfaction, Burnout, and Turnover in Health Care Social Workers," *Health and Social Work* 16 (1991): 193–202; John Poulin and Carolyn Walter, "Social Worker Burnout: A Longitudinal Study," *Social Work Research and Abstracts* 29 (1993): 5–11; Myung-Yong Um and Dianne F. Harrison, "Role Stressors, Burnout, Mediators, and Job Satisfaction," *Social Work Research* 22:2 (1998): 100–115; Chris Lloyd, Robert King, and Lesley Chenoweth, "Social Work, Stress and Burnout: A Review," *Journal of Mental Health* 11 (2002): 255–65.

8. See Peter Vogt, "Fight Burnout: Tips for Caring for Yourself," http://216.239.37.104/search?q=cache:weJL0EbjrUwJ:healthcare.monster.com/socs/articles/burnout/+burnout+social+workers&hl=en&ie=UTF-8. Date accessed: August 6, 2003.

9. See, for example, S. R. Rose and K. L. DeWeaver, "Part-Time and Full-Time MSW Enrollment Intentions and Interests of Professionals and Social Work Students," *Journal of Continuing Social Work Education* 5 (1992): 15–20; A. C. Butler, "A Reevaluation of Social Work Students' Career Interests," *Journal of Social Work Education* 26 (1990): 45–56; R. Kats, S. Sharlin, and N. Nahmani, "Staying or Leaving? The Commitment of Social Workers to Their Work," *British Journal of Social Work* 23 (1987): 449–58.

10. Maynard-Moody and Musheno, *Cops, Teachers, Counselors*, 157.

11. See Thomas L. Gais, "Welfare Reform: Findings in Brief" (Albany, NY: The Nelson A. Rockefeller Institute of Government, March 2002); and Rockefeller Institute of Government, *2001 Annual Report: Federalism Research Group* (Albany, NY: The Nelson A. Rockefeller Institute of Government, 2001).

Chapter 7. How Public Management Matters

1. Mary Jo Bane and David T. Ellwood, *Welfare Realities: From Rhetoric to Reform* (Cambridge, MA: Harvard University Press, 1994).

2. Thomas L. Gais, "Welfare Reform: Findings in Brief" (Albany, NY: The

Nelson A. Rockefeller Institute of Government, March 2002), 3, emphasis in original. See also Rockefeller Institute of Government, *2001 Annual Report: Federalism Research Group* (Albany, NY: The Nelson A. Rockefeller Institute of Government, 2001).

3. Hugh Heclo, *Government of Strangers* (Washington, D.C.: Brookings Institution, 1977). Herbert Kaufman, *Red Tape: Its Origins, Uses, and Abuses* (Washington, D.C.: Brookings Institution, 1977); Herbert Kaufman, *The Administrative Behavior of Federal Bureau Chiefs* (Washington, D.C.: Brookings Institution, 1981).

4. Ralph P. Hummel, *The Bureaucratic Experience,* 4th edition (New York: St. Martin's Press, 1994), vii.

5. Thomas L. Gais discusses the more salient role that executive branches of state governments played in delivering welfare reform as compared with state legislatures. "Concluding Comments: Welfare Reform and Governance," in Carol S. Weissert (ed.), *Learning from Leaders* (Albany, NY: The Rockefeller Institute Press, 2000), 173–89.

6. Rockefeller Institute of Government, *2001 Annual Report*, 2.

7. Ibid.

8. Gais, "Welfare Reform," 1. See also Thomas L. Gais and Kent Weaver, "State Policy Choices under TANF," in Ron Haskins, Andrea Kane, Isabel V. Sawhill, and Kent R. Weaver (eds.), *Welfare Reform and Beyond: The Future of the Safety Net* (Washington, DC: Brookings Institution, 2002. Also reprinted in Brookings Institution Policy Brief No. 21, April 2002); Richard P. Nathan and Thomas L. Gais, *Implementing The Personal Responsibility Act of 1996: A First Look* (Albany, NY: The Nelson A. Rockefeller Institute of Government, 1999).

9. Evelyn Z. Brodkin, "Requiem for Welfare," *Dissent* 50 (2003): 29–36, quotation 29.

10. Brodkin, "Requiem for Welfare."

11. Gais, "Welfare Reform," 4.

12. See Sharon Parrott, "Welfare Recipients Who Find Jobs: What Do We Know About Their Employment and Earnings?" (Washington, D.C.: Center on Budget and Policy Priorities, November 16, 1998), http://www.cbpp.org/11-16-98wel.htm. Date accessed: June 5, 2003.

13. Institute for Women's Policy Research, "Before and After Welfare Reform: The Work and Well-Being of Low-Income Single Parent Families," Fact Sheet (Washington, D.C.: The Institute for Women's Policy Research, June 2003). The report is available at http://www.iwpr.org/pdf/WWVI.pdf. Date accessed: June 15, 2003. See also the many studies produced by the Urban Institute, accessible at http://www.urban.org.

14. Institute for Women's Policy Research, "Before and After Welfare Reform."

15. Cynthia Miller, *Leavers, Stayers, and Cyclers: An Analysis of the Welfare Caseload* (New York: MDRC, November 2002), 5. See also Gayle Hamilton, *Moving People from Welfare to Work: Lessons from the National Evaluation of Welfare-to-Work Strategies* (New York: MDRC, July 2002).

16. Brodkin, "Requiem for Welfare."

17. See, for example, Children's Defense Fund, "TANF Reauthorization: A Side-by-Side Comparison of the Proposals Before Congress," July 2003, http://www.childrensdefense.org/fs_tanf_reauthprops.php+TANF+2003+ reauthorization+proposals&hl=en&ie=UTF-8. Date accessed: September 9, 2003. And also, Children's Defense Fund, "President Bush's Welfare Reform Plan Leaves Millions of Children Behind," July 2003, http://www.childrensdefense .org/fs_bushwelfplan.php. Date accessed: September 9, 2003.

References

Allen, L. "The Engineered Communication." Professional Communication Conference, October 30–November 1, 1991. *Proceedings*, volume 2, 351–55.

Bane, Mary Jo. "Welfare Reform and Mandatory Versus Voluntary Work: Policy Issue or Management Problem?" *Journal of Policy Analysis and Management* 8:2 (1989): 285–89.

Bane, Mary Jo, and David T. Ellwood *Welfare Realities: From Rhetoric to Reform.* Cambridge, MA: Harvard University Press, 1994.

Bardach, Eugene. *Improving the Productivity of JOBS Programs.* New York: MDRC, 1993.

Barnard, Chester. *The Functions of the Executive.* Cambridge, MA: Harvard University Press, 1938.

Behn, Robert D. "What Right do Public Managers Have to Lead?" *Public Administration Review* 58:3 (May/June 1998): 209–25.

———. "Creating an Innovative Organization: Ten Hints for Involving Frontline Workers." *State and Local Government Review* 27:3 (1995): 221–34.

———. *Leadership Counts.* Cambridge, MA: Harvard University Press, 1991.

Brehm, John, and Scott Gates. *Working, Shirking and Sabotage: Bureaucratic Response to a Democratic Public.* Ann Arbor: University of Michigan Press, 1997.

Brodkin, Evelyn Z. "Requiem for Welfare." *Dissent*, 50:1 (2003): 29–36.

Brudney, Jeffrey L., Laurence J. O'Toole Jr., and Hal G. Rainey. *Advancing Public Management: New Developments in Theory, Methods, and Practice.* Washington, D.C.: Georgetown University Press, 2000.

Burke, Ronald J. "Management Practices, Employees' Satisfaction and Perceptions of Quality Service." *Psychological Reports* 77:3 (1995): 748–50.

Butler, A. C. "A Reevaluation of Social Work Students' Career Interests." *Journal of Social Work Education* 26:1 (1990): 45–56.

Carroll, James D. "The Rhetoric of Reform and Political Reality in the National Performance Review." *Public Administration Review* 55:3 (1995): 302–12.

Children's Defense Fund. "President Bush's Welfare Reform Plan Leaves Millions of Children Behind." July 2003, http://www.childrensdefense.org/fs_bushwelfplan.php. Date accessed: 09/09/03.

———. "TANF Reauthorization: A Side-by-Side Comparison of the Proposals before Congress." July 2003, http://www.childrensdefense.org/fs _tanf_reauthprops.php+TANF+2003+reauthorization+proposals&hl =en&ie=UTF-8. Date accessed: 09/09/03.

Clark-Daniels, Carolyn L., and R. Steven Daniels. "Street-Level Decision Making in Elder Mistreatment Policy: An Empirical Case Study of Service Rationing." *Social Science Quarterly* 76:3 (1995): 460–73.

Coggburn, Jerrell D., and Saundra K. Schneider. "The Quality of Management and Government Performance: An Empirical Analysis of the American States." *Public Administration Review* 63:2 (2003): 206–13.

Cohen, Steven A. "Defining and Measuring Effectiveness in Public Management." *Public Productivity and Management Review* 17:1 (1993): 45–57.

Cohen, Steven A., and William Eimicke. *The New Effective Public Manager.* San Francisco: Jossey-Bass, 1995.

Crook, Wendy P. "Trickle-Down Bureaucracy: Does the Organization Affect Client Responses to Programs?" *Administration in Social Work* 26:1 (2001): 37–59.

Dellinger, Kirsten. "Wearing Gender and Sexuality 'On Your Sleeve': Dress Norms and the Importance of Occupational and Organizational Culture at Work." *Gender Issues* 20:1 (2002): 3–25.

Denhardt, Janet Vinzant, and Robert B. Denhardt. *Creating a Culture of Innovation: 10 Lessons from America's Best Run City.* Arlington, VA: PricewaterhouseCoopers Endowment for the Business of Government, 2001.

Denhardt, Robert B. *The Pursuit of Significance: Strategies for Managerial Success in Public Organizations.* Belmont, CA: Wadsworth Publishing, 1993.

Denhardt, Robert B., and Janet Vinzant Denhardt. *Leadership for Change: Case Studies in American Local Government.* Arlington, VA: Pricewaterhouse-Coopers Endowment for the Business of Government, 1999.

Eckstrom, Elizabeth, and David M. Buchner. "Changing Physician Practice of Physical Activity Counseling." *Journal of General Internal Medicine* 14:6 (1999): 376–78.

Elmore, Richard F. "Backward Mapping: Implementation Research and Policy Decisions." *Political Science Quarterly* 94:4 (1979–80): 601–16.

Follett, Mary Parker. *Creative Experience.* New York: Longmans, Green Publishers, 1924.

———. *The New State: Group Organization, the Solution of Popular Government.* New York: Longmans, Green Publishers, 1918.

Frederickson, H. George. *The Spirit of Public Administration.* San Francisco: Jossey-Bass, 1997.

Frederickson, H. George, and Kevin B. Smith. *The Public Administration Theory Primer.* Boulder, CO: Westview Press, 2003.

Gais, Thomas L. "Welfare Reform: Findings in Brief." Albany, NY: The Nelson A. Rockefeller Institute of Government, March 2002.

———. "Concluding Comments: Welfare Reform and Governance." In Carol S. Weissert (ed.), *Learning from Leaders*. Albany, NY: The Rockefeller Institute Press, 2000. 173–89.

Gais, Thomas L., and Richard P. Nathan. *Status Report on the Occasion of the 5th Anniversary of the 1996 Personal Responsibility Welfare-Reform Act*. Albany, NY: The Nelson A. Rockefeller Institute of Government, August 2001.

Gais, Thomas L., and Kent Weaver. "State Policy Choices Under TANF." In Ron Haskins, Andrea Kane, Isabel V. Sawhill, and Kent R. Weaver (eds.), *Welfare Reform and Beyond: The Future of the Safety Net*. Washington, D.C.: Brookings Institution, 2002. (Also reprinted in Brookings Institution Policy Brief No. 21.)

Goodsell, Charles. "Reinventing Government or Rediscovering It?" *Public Administration Review* 53 (January/February 1993): 85–86.

———. "Looking Once Again at Human Service Bureaucracy." *Journal of Politics* 43:1 (1981): 763–78.

———. "Client Evaluation of Three Welfare Programs." *Administration and Society* 12 (1980): 123–36.

Greco, P. J., and J. M. Eisenberg. "Changing Physicians' Practices." *The New England Journal of Medicine* 329:17 (1993): 1271–74.

Guthrie, James P. "High-Involvement Work Practices, Turnover, and Productivity: Evidence from New Zealand." *Academy of Management Journal* 44:1 (2001): 180–92.

Hall, D. L., and A. Nauda. "Management through the Year 2000: Gaining the Competitive Advantage." Institute of Electrical and Electronics Engineers (IEEE), Engineering Management Conference, October 21–24, 1990. 153–58.

Hamilton, Gayle. *Moving People from Welfare to Work: Lessons from the National Evaluation of Welfare-to-Work Strategies*. New York: MDRC, July 2002.

Handler, J. F. *The Conditions of Discretion: Autonomy, Community, Bureaucracy*. New York: Russell Sage, 1986.

Hasenfeld, Yeheskel. "Organizational Forms as Moral Practices: The Case of Welfare Departments." *Social Service Review* 74:3 (2000): 329–51.

———. "Social Services and Welfare-to-Work: Prospects for the Social Work Profession." *Administration in Social Work* 23:3/4 (2000): 185–99.

———. (ed.). *Human Services as Complex Organizations*. Newbury Park, CA: Sage, 1992.

Heclo, Hugh. *Government of Strangers*. Washington, D.C.: Brookings Institution, 1977.

Heinrich, Carolyn J., and Laurence E. Lynn Jr. "Government and Performance: The Influence of Programs Structure and Management on Job Training Partnership Act (JTPA) Program Outcomes." In Carolyn Heinrich and Laurence E. Lynn Jr. (eds.), *Governance and Performance: New Perspectives*. Washington, D.C.: Georgetown University Press, 2000.

Herzberg, Frederick. *Work and the Nature of Man*. New York: Mentor Executive Library, 1966.

Heskett, James L., W. Earl Sasser, and Christopher W. L. Hart. *Service Breakthroughs*. New York: Free Press, 1990.

Hummel, Ralph P. *The Bureaucratic Experience*. 4th edition. New York: St. Martin's Press, 1994.

Hutchison, Steven, Kathleen E. Valentino, and Sandra L. Kirkner. "What Works for the Gander Does Not Work as Well for the Goose: The Effects of Leader Behavior." *Journal of Applied Social Psychology* 28:2 (1998): 171–83.

Ichniowski, Casey, Kathryn Shaw, and Giovanna Prennushi. "The Effects of Human Resource Management Practices on Productivity: A Study of Steel Finishing Lines." *American Economic Review* 87:3 (1997): 291–314.

IIE (Institute of Industrial Engineers). "Cynical Employees Created by Bad Management." *Solutions Magazine* 32:12 (2000): 74.

Imbornoni, Ann-Marie. "George Walker Bush. A Son of a President, Now President." January 15, 2001. http://www.factmonster.com/index.html. Date accessed: 06/01/03.

Ingraham, Patricia W., and Amy Kneedler Donahue. "Dissecting the Black Box Revisited: Characterizing Government Management Capacity." In Carolyn J. Heinrich and Laurence E. Lynn Jr. (eds.), *Governance and Performance: New Perspectives*. Washington, D.C.: Georgetown University Press, 2000, 292–318.

Ingraham, Patricia W., James R. Thompson, and Ronald P. Sanders. *Transforming Government*. San Francisco: Jossey-Bass Publishers, 1998.

Ingraham, Patricia W., Philip G. Joyce, and Amy Kneedler Donahue. *Government Performance: Why Management Matters*. Baltimore: Johns Hopkins University Press, 2003.

IWPR. The Institute for Women's Policy Research. "Before and After Welfare Reform: The Work and Well-Being of Low-Income Single Parent Families." Fact Sheet. Washington, D.C.: The Institute for Women's Policy Research, June 2003. www.iwpr.org/pdf/WWVI.pdf. Date accessed: 06/15/03.

Jennings, Edward T., Jr., and Jo Ann G. Ewalt. "Interorganizational Coordination, Administrative Consolidation, and Policy Performance." *Public Administration Review* 58:5 (1998): 417–28.

Johnston, Jocelyn J., and Cherita L. McIntyre. "Organizational Culture and Climate Correlates of Job Satisfaction." *Psychological Reports* 82:3 (1998): 851–60.

Kamensky, John M. "The Role of 'Re-inventing Government' in Federal Management Reform." *Public Administration Review* 56:3 (1996): 247–55.

Kane, Thomas J., and Mary Jo Bane. *Welfare Realities: From Rhetoric to Reform.* Cambridge, MA: Harvard University Press, 1994.

Kats, R., S. Sharlin, and N. Nahmani. "Staying or Leaving? The Commitment of Social Workers to Their Work." *British Journal of Social Work* 23:2 (1987): 449–58.

Kaufman, Herbert. *The Administrative Behavior of Federal Bureau Chiefs.* Washington, D.C.: Brookings Institution, 1981.

———. *Red Tape: Its Origins, Uses, and Abuses.* Washington, D.C.: Brookings Institution, 1977.

Keiser, Lael R. "State Bureaucratic Discretion and the Administration of Social Welfare Programs: The Case of Social Security Disability." *Journal of Public Administration Research and Theory* 9:1 (1999): 87–107.

Keiser, Lael R., Vicky M. Wilkins, Kenneth J. Meier, and Catherine Holland. "Lipstick and Logarithms: Gender, Institutional Context, and Representative Bureaucracy." *American Political Science Review* 96:3 (2002): 553–64.

Kelly, Marisa. "Theories of Justice and Street-Level Discretion." *Journal of Public Administration Research and Theory* 4:2 (1994): 119–40.

Kettl, Donald F. "The Global Revolution in Public Management: Driving Themes, Missing Links." *Journal of Policy Analysis and Management* 16:3 (1997): 446–62.

Khademian, Anne M. "Is Silly Putty Manageable? Looking for the Links between Culture, Management, and Context." In Jeffrey L. Brudney, Laurence J. O'Toole Jr., and Hal G. Rainey (eds.), *Advancing Public Management.* Washington, D.C.: Georgetown University Press, 2000. 33–48.

Kilman, R. H., M. J. Saxton, and R. Serpa. "Issues in Understanding and Changing Culture." *California Management Review* 28:2 (1986): 87–94.

Komaki, Judith L. "Toward Effective Supervision: An Operant Analysis and Comparison of Managers at Work." *Journal of Applied Psychology* 71:2 (1986): 270–80.

Lawler, Edward E., III, and Lyman W. Porter. "The Effect of Performance on Job Satisfaction." *Industrial Relations* 7:1 (1967): 20–28.

Light, Paul C. "Does Management Matter?" *Governing Magazine.* February 1, 1999, http://www.govexec.com/gpp/0299publicservice.htm. Date accessed: 06/10/03.

Lin, Ann Chih. *Reform in the Making: The Implementation of Social Policy in Prison.* Princeton, NJ: Princeton University Press, 2000.

Lipsky, Michael. "Bureaucratic Disentitlement in Social Welfare Programs." *Social Service Review* 58:1 (1984): 3–27.

————. *Street Level Bureaucrats: Dilemmas of the Individual in Public Services*, New York: Russell Sage, 1980.

Lloyd, Chris, Robert King, and Lesley Chenoweth. "Social Work, Stress and Burnout: A Review." *Journal of Mental Health* 11:3 (2002): 255–65.

Lundberg, George D. "Changing Physician Behavior in Ordering Diagnostic Tests." *Journal of the American Medical Association* (JAMA) 280:23 (1998): 2036.

Lurie, Irene, and Norma M. Riccucci. "Changing the 'Culture' of Welfare Offices: From Vision to the Front Lines." *Administration and Society* 34:6 (2003): 653–77.

Lynn, Laurence E., Jr. "The Myth of the Bureaucratic Paradigm: What Traditional Public Administration Stood For." *Public Administration Review* 61:2 (2001): 144–60.

————. *Public Management as Art, Science, and Profession*. Chatham, NJ: Chatham House Publishers, Inc, 1996.

————. *Managing Public Policy*. Boston: Little, Brown and Co., 1987.

————. "The Reagan Administration and the Renitent Bureaucracy," in Lester M. Salamon and Michael S. Lund (eds.), *The Reagan Presidency and the Governing of America*. Washington, D.C.: Urban Institute, 1984. 339–70.

Malka, S. "Managerial Behavior, Participation, and Effectiveness in Social Welfare Organizations." *Administration in Social Work* 13:2 (1989): 47–65.

Maynard-Moody, Steven, and Michael C. Musheno. *Cops, Teachers, Counselors: Stories from the Front Lines of Public Service*. Ann Arbor: University of Michigan Press, 2003.

————. "State Agent or Citizen Agent: Two Narratives of Discretion." *Journal of Public Administration Research and Theory* 10:2 (2000): 329–58.

Mead, Lawrence M. "Welfare Caseload Change: An Alternative Approach." *Policy Studies Journal* 31:2 (2003): 163–85.

————. "Caseload Change: An Exploratory Study." *Journal of Policy Analysis and Management* 19:3 (2000): 465–72.

————. "The Decline of Welfare in Wisconsin." *Journal of Public Administration Research and Theory* 9:4 (1999): 597–622.

Meier, Kenneth J. "Latinos and Representative Bureaucracy: Testing the Thompson and Henderson Hypotheses." *Journal of Public Administration Research and Theory* 3:4 (1993): 393–415.

Meier, Kenneth J., and John Bohte. "Structure and Discretion: Missing Links in Representative Bureaucracy." *Journal of Public Administration Research and Theory* 11:4 (2001): 455–70.

Meier, Kenneth J., and Laurence J. O'Toole Jr. "Public Management and Organizational Performance: The Effect of Managerial Quality." *Journal of Public Administration Research and Theory* 12:4 (2002): 629–43.

————. "Managerial Strategies and Behavior in Networks: A Model with Evidence from U.S. Public Education." *Journal of Public Administration Research and Theory* 11:3 (2001): 271–93.

Meyers, Marcia K., and Nara Dillon. "Institutional Paradoxes: Why Welfare Workers Can't Reform Welfare." In H. George Frederickson and Jocelyn M. Johnston (eds.), *Public Administration Reform and Innovation*. Tuscaloosa: University of Alabama Press, 1999. 230–58.

Meyers, Marcia K., Bonnie Glaser, and Karin MacDonald. "On the Front Lines of Welfare Delivery: Are Workers Implementing Policy Reforms?" *Journal of Policy Analysis and Management* 17:1 (1998): 1–22.

Meyers, Marcia K., and Susan Vorsanger. "Street-Level Bureaucrats and the Implementation of Public Policy." In B. Guy Peters and Jon Pierre (eds.), *Handbook of Public Administration*. Thousand Oaks, CA: Sage Publications, 2003, 245–55.

Miller, Cynthia. *Leavers, Stayers, and Cyclers: An Analysis of the Welfare Caseload*. New York: MDRC, November 2002.

Milward, H. Brinton, and Keith G. Provan. "Principles for Controlling Agents: The Political Economy of Network Structures." *Journal of Public Administration Research and Theory* 8:2 (1998): 203–22.

Moe, Ronald C. "The 'Reinventing Government' Exercise: Misinterpreting the Problem, Misjudging the Consequences." *Public Administration Review* 54 (March/April 1994): 111–22.

Moore, Mark. *Creating Public Value*. Cambridge, MA: Harvard University Press, 1997.

Morgan, Douglas, et al. 1996. "What Middle Managers Do in Local Government." *Public Administration Review* 56:4 (1997): 359–66.

Mosher, Frederick C. *Democracy and the Public Service*. New York: Oxford University Press, 1968.

Nachmias, David, and David H. Rosenbloom. *Bureaucratic Government, USA*. New York: St. Martin's Press, 1980.

Nakamura, Robert T., and Frank Smallwood. *The Politics of Policy Implementation*. New York: St. Martin's Press, 1980.

Nathan, Richard P., and Thomas L. Gais. *Implementing The Personal Responsibility Act of 1996: A First Look*. Albany, NY: The Nelson A. Rockefeller Institute of Government, 1999.

Nystrom, H. E. "Teaching and Learning in an Era of Change." Frontiers in Education Conference, 27th annual conference, November 5–8, 1997. *Proceedings*, volume 2, 812–14.

Osborne, David, and Ted Gaebler. *Reinventing Government: How the Entrepreneurial Spirit Is Transforming the Public Sector*. New York: Plume, 1993.

————. *Reinventing Government*. Reading, MA: Addison-Wesley, 1992.

O'Toole, Laurence J., Jr., and Kenneth J. Meier. "Networks, Hierarchies, and Public Management: Modeling and Nonlinearities." In Carolyn Heinrich and Laurence E. Lynn Jr. (eds.), *Governance and Performance: New Perspectives*. Washington, D.C.: Georgetown University Press, 2000.

Parrott, Sharon. "Welfare Recipients Who Find Jobs: What Do We Know about Their Employment and Earnings?" Washington, D.C.: Center on Budget and Policy Priorities, November 16, 1998. www.cbpp.org/11-16-98wel .htm. Date accessed: 06/05/03.

Pavetti, LaDonna A. "Welfare Policy in Transition: Redefining the Social Contract for Poor Citizen Families with Children and for Immigrants." In S. H. Danziger and R. H. Haveman (eds.), *Understanding Poverty*. New York: Russell Sage Foundation, 2001. 229–77.

Paviour, R. "The Influence of Class and Race on Clinical Assessments by MSW Students." *Social Service Review* 62:4 (1988): 684–93.

Pesso, T. "Local Welfare Offices: Managing the Intake Process." *Public Policy* 26:2 (1978), 305–30.

Porter, Lyman W., and Edward E. Lawler III. *Managerial Attitudes and Performance*. Homewood, IL: Richard D. Irwin, 1968.

Poulin, John, and Carolyn Walter. "Social Worker Burnout: A Longitudinal Study." *Social Work Research and Abstracts* 29:4 (1993): 5–11.

Prottas, Jeffrey Manditch. *People-Processing: The Street-Level Bureaucrat in Public Service Bureaucracies*. Lexington, MA: Lexington Books, 1979.

Radin, Beryl A. *The Accountable Juggler: The Art of Leadership in a Federal Agency*. Washington, D.C.: Congressional Quarterly Press, 2002.

————. *Beyond Machiavelli: Policy Analysis Comes of Age*. Washington, D.C.: Georgetown University Press, 2000.

Rainey, Hal G. *Understanding and Managing Public Organizations*. San Francisco: Jossey-Bass, 1997.

Rainey, Hal G., and Paula Steinbauer. "Galloping Elephants: Developing Elements of a Theory of Effective Government Organizations." *Journal of Public Administration Research and Theory* 9:1 (1999): 1–32.

Ramsdell, P. S. "Staff Participation in Organizational Decision-Making: An Empirical Study." *Administration in Social Work* 18:4 (1994): 51–71.

Recesso, Arthur, M. "First Year Implementation of the School to Work Opportunities Act Policy: An Effort at Backward Mapping." *Education Policy Analysis Archives* 7:11 (1999).

Riccucci, Norma M. *Unsung Heroes: Federal Execucrats Making a Difference*. Washington, D.C.: Georgetown University Press, 1996.

Riccucci, Norma M., and Judith R. Saidel. "The Representativeness of State-

Level Bureaucratic Leaders: A Missing Piece of the Representative Bureaucracy Puzzle." *Public Administration Review* 57:5 (1997): 423–30.

Riccucci, Norma M., Marcia K. Meyers, Irene Lurie, and Jun Seop Han. "The Implementation of Welfare Reform Policy: The Role of Public Managers in Front-Line Practices." *Public Administration Review* 64 (2004): 438–48.

Rockefeller Institute of Government. *2001 Annual Report: Federalism Research Group*. Albany, NY: The Nelson A. Rockefeller Institute of Government, 2001.

Rose, S. R., and K. L. De Weaver. "Part-Time and Full-Time MSW Enrollment Intentions and Interests of Professionals and Social Work Students." *Journal of Continuing Social Work Education* 5:3 (1992): 15–20.

Rosenbloom, David H. *Public Administration: Understanding Management, Politics and Law in the Public Sector*. 4th edition. New York: McGraw-Hill, 1998.

Rosenbloom, David H., Robert S. Kravchuk, and Deborah Goldman Rosenbloom. *Public Administration: Understanding Management, Politics, and Law in the Public Sector*. 5th edition. New York: McGraw-Hill, 2002.

Rothlisberger, Fritz J., and William J. Diskson. *Management and the Worker: An Account of Research Conducted by the Western Electric Company, Hawthorne Works, Chicago*. Cambridge, MA: Harvard University Press, 1967.

Rourke, Francis E. *Bureaucracy, Politics and Public Policy*. 2nd edition. Boston: Little, Brown and Co., 1976.

Sagie, Abraham, and Jacob Weisberg. "A Structural Analysis of Behavior in Work Situations Shared by Group Members." *Journal of Psychology* 130:4 (1996): 371–81.

Sandfort, Jodi R. "Moving beyond Discretion and Outcomes: Examining Public Management from the Front Lines of the Welfare System." *Journal of Public Administration Research and Theory* 10:4 (2000): 729–56.

———. "The Structural Impediments of Human Service Collaboration: The Case of Front-Line Welfare Reform Implementation." *Social Service Review* 73:3 (1999): 314–39.

Sayre, Wallace. "The Triumph of Techniques over Purpose." *Public Administration Review* 8:2 (1948): 134–37.

Schein, Edgar H. *Organizational Culture and Leadership*, 2nd edition. San Francisco: Jossey-Bass, 1992.

———. "What You Need to Know about Organizational Culture." *Training and Development Journal*, 40:1 (1986): 30–33.

Schneider, Saundra K., and William G. Jacoby. "Influences on Bureaucratic Policy Initiatives in the American States." *Journal of Public Administration Research and Theory* 6:4 (1996): 495–522.

Schneider, Saundra K., William G. Jacoby, and Jerrell D. Coggburn. "The

Structure of Bureaucratic Decisions in the American States." *Public Administration Review* 57:3 (1997): 240–49.

Schorr, Alvin L. *Welfare Reform: Failure and Remedies.* Westport, CT: Praeger Publishers, 2001.

Scott, Patrick G. "Assessing Determinants of Bureaucratic Discretion: An Experiment in Street-Level Decision Making." *Journal of Public Administration Research and Theory* 7:1 (1997): 35–57.

Shaw, W. H., and T. R. Manley. "Managing in a Global Environment." Institute of Electrical and Electronics Engineers (IEEE), Engineering Management Conference, October 25-28, 1992. 106–10.

Siefert, Kristine, and Srinika Jayaratne. "Job Satisfaction, Burnout, and Turnover in Health Care Social Workers." *Health and Social Work* 16:3 (1991): 193–202.

Solomon, Daniel H., Hideki Hashimoto, Lawren Daltroy, and Matthew H. Liang. "Techniques to Improve Physicians' Use of Diagnostic Tests: A New Conceptual Framework." *Journal of the American Medical Association* (JAMA) 280:23 (1998): 2020–27.

State Capacity Report, Michigan. Albany, NY: The Nelson A. Rockefeller Institute of Government, 1998.

State Capacity Report, Texas. Albany, NY: The Nelson A. Rockefeller Institute of Government, 1998.

State Capacity Report, Georgia. Albany, NY: The Nelson A. Rockefeller Institute of Government, 1998.

State Capacity Report, New York. Albany, NY: The Nelson A. Rockefeller Institute of Government, 1998.

Stone, C. N. "Attitudinal Tendencies among Officials." In Charles Goodsell (ed.), *The Public Encounter: Where State and Citizen Meet.* Bloomington: Indiana University Press, 1981.

Terry, Larry D. *Leadership of Public Bureaucracies: The Administrator as Conservator.* Thousand Oaks, CA: Sage Publications, 1995.

Trice, Harrison M. *Occupational Subcultures in the Workplace.* Ithaca, NY: Industrial and Labor Relations Press, 1993.

Trice, Harrison M., and Janice M. Beyer. *The Culture of Work Organizations.* Englewood Cliffs, NJ: Prentice Hall, 1992.

Um, Myung-Yong, and Dianne F. Harrison. "Role Stressors, Burnout, Mediators, and Job Satisfaction." *Social Work Research* 22:2 (1998): 100–115.

U.S. Department of Health and Human Services (HHS). *Temporary Assistance for Needy Families (TANF) Program.* Washington, D.C.: U.S. HHS, August 1998.

U.S. General Accounting Office (GAO). *States Are Restructuring Programs to Reduce Welfare Dependence*. Washington, D.C.: U.S. GAO, June 1998.

Vinzant, Janet Coble, and Lane Crothers. *Street-Level Leadership: Discretion and Legitimacy in Front-Line Public Service*. Washington, D.C.: Georgetown University Press, 1998.

Wagner, John A., III, and Jeffrey A. LePine. "Effects of Participation on Performance and Satisfaction: Additional Meta-analytic Evidence." *Psychological Reports* 84:3 (1999): 719–26.

Waldo, Dwight. *The Enterprise of Public Administration*. Novato, CA: Chandler and Sharp Publishers, Inc., 1980.

Wang, Thomas J., Elizabeth Mort, Paul Nordberg, Yuchiao Chang, Mary Cadigan, Laura Mylott, Lillian Ananian, B. Taylor Thompson, Michael Fessler, Willian Warren, Amy Wheeler, Mark Jordan, and Michael Fifer. "A Utilization Management Intervention to Reduce Unnecessary Testing in the Coronary Care Unit." *Archives of Internal Medicine* 162:16 (2002): 1885–90.

Weatherley, R. A. "Participating Management in Public Welfare: What Are the Prospects?" *Administration in Social Work* 7:1 (1983): 39–49.

Weissert, Carol S. "Beyond the Organization: The Influence of Community and Personal Values on Street-Level Bureaucrats' Responsiveness." *Journal of Public Administration Research and Theory* 4:2 (1994): 225–55.

Wexley, Kenneth N., and Gary A. Yukl. *Organization Behavior and Personnel Psychology*. Revised edition. Homewood, IL: Richard D. Irwin, Inc., 1984.

Wilson, James Q. *Bureaucracy: What Government Agencies Do and Why They Do It*. New York: Basic Books, 1989.

Zedlewski, Sheila R., and Jennifer Holland. *How Much Do Welfare Recipients Know about Time Limits?* Washington, D.C.: Urban Institute, December 2003.

Index